ADHD in the Young Child

Cathy L. Reimers, Ph.D.
Bruce A. Brunger

Illustrated by
Bruce A. Brunger

Specialty Press, Inc.
300 N.W. 70th Ave., Suite 102
Plantation, Florida 33317

ISBN 1-886941-32-7

Library of Congress Cataloging-in-Publication Data

Reimers, Cathy L., 1954–
        ADHD in the young child driven to re-direction: a guide for
parents and teachers of young children with ADHD : a book for parents
and teachers / Cathy L. Reimers, Bruce A. Brunger ;
illustrated by Bruce A. Brunger.
            p.   cm.
    Includes bibliographical references and index.
    ISBN 1-886941-32-7
    1. Attention-deficit-disordered children.   2. Attention-deficit
hyperactivity disorder--Treatment. 3. Hyperactive children.
I. Brunger, Bruce A.,   1961–   . II. Title.
RJ506.H9R45   1999
618.92' 8589--dc21   99-38801
                                                            CIP

Cover Design by Bruce A. Brunger
Illustrated by Bruce A. Brunger

10 9 8 7 6 5 4 3 2 1

Printed in the United States of America

Specialty Press, Inc.
300 Northwest 70th Avenue, Suite 102
Plantation, Florida 33317
(954) 792-8100 • (800) 233-9273
www.addwarehouse.com

Dedication

To Keiko, who always wanted a book like this,
and whose patience allowed it to be written.

To Kenny, the inspiration for Buzz.
To his little brother, Mikey
and to his little sister, Lisa.

To Emilie, the inspiration for Pixie.
And finally, to Erik and his pretend friend.

Table of Contents

Why We Wrote This Book

Parenting always has its challenges. However, the challenge is even greater with a child who has been diagnosed with Attention Deficit Hyperactivity Disorder (ADHD).

Researchers have found that characteristics of ADHD can be identified even before the age of three. However, often it is not diagnosed until much later in the child's elementary school years. If your child's ADHD is diagnosed early, you have the advantage of dealing with it sooner.

You are probably reading this because as a parent you have a child diagnosed with ADHD, or as a teacher you have one or more children with ADHD in your classroom. If you are like us, you have probably searched in vain for a book that would help you understand what ADHD is and how you can deal with it at home, at school, or in other places. While you may have found some general information about ADHD in older children and adults, you have probably discovered that there seems to be little helpful information on young children with ADHD. You may have read reams of books and stacks of reports, spent hours talking with friends or attending support groups, visited numerous bookstores and perhaps even searched the Internet.

You have probably wondered why there was not some kind of one-stop reference book about ADHD in young children. One that is easy to understand and serves as a handy, interactive guide. Until now, there was no such book. That's why we wrote *ADHD in the Young Child.*

In this book we examine young children who have the symptoms of ADHD. We offer parents and teachers of ADHD children many effective techniques to manage behavior. We hope this book will prove itself invaluable.

The idea for this book began when I met Bruce Brunger and his wife, Keiko, to discuss my observations of their son, Kenny. Kenny had been exhibiting ADHD behavior in school, and I was asked to observe him on several occasions in school.

In the course of our discussions, Bruce and Keiko showed me how they worked with Kenny to help him remember and model appropriate behavior at school. One of the techniques they developed was a cartoon book, drawn by Bruce, depicting various school situations with Kenny as the star character. Each cartoon panel showed a before-and-after situation in which Kenny was first misbehaving and then later acting appropriately. Bruce and Keiko would review the book with Kenny each morning before he went to school to reinforce the concepts with him. As a result of the custom made cartoon book, Kenny was visualizing the examples of appropriate behavior, and learned to recognize and avoid the misbehaviors depicted in the book.

We also discussed the difficulty in obtaining information on how to deal with young children with ADHD. We decided to join forces and write this book.

I am a clinical psychologist in private practice, specializing in child psychology. Building on my training at Nova Southeastern University in Ft. Lauderdale, Florida, I have actively pursued my interest in developmental child psychology. I have performed evaluations for children in early childhood programs such as Head Start, public preschools and elementary schools, and have also administered testing for the North County Mental Health of San Mateo County, California. I have observed, evaluated, and worked with a number of ADHD children during the past 15 years. As the parent of an ADHD child, I also identify and have struggled with the mixed emotions, the frustration, and the exhaustion of living with the daily demands of a young child with ADHD.

A great deal of research and hard work went into the development of this book. In addition to my work with ADHD children, I have spent years examining the volumes of research completed in this field. We have summarized the most relevant findings in this book for your understanding and benefit.

In my counseling work with ADHD children, I found that the feelings and needs of the parents and teachers of these children must be considered. Throughout this book, I balance the treatment of the children with a view of the feelings of the adults who interact with them.

I want to introduce to parents and teachers the concept of redirection. By "redirection," I am saying that we, as parents and teachers, need to modify our attitudes and our emotional responses to the child's behavior.

This book would not be possible without my co-author Bruce A. Brunger, whose original work, creativity, artistic talents, and ideas have helped shape the content and practical nature of this book.

I also wish to thank my professor, Dr. Marilyn Segal, Ph. D., Director of the Family Center at Nova Southeastern University and Dr. Harry Verby, M.D., pediatrician, for their constructive review of this text.

Finally, I express my appreciation to the Head Start Program of San Mateo County, for allowing me to field-test the techniques in this book.

We and the publisher, Specialty Press, endeavored to make *ADHD in the Young Child* the most complete and useful guide of its kind for the parent and teacher of the young child with ADHD. We welcome your comments and suggestions.

Cathy L. Reimers, Ph.D.

Introduction

Try to imagine what it takes to control our behavior. We take for granted the ability to stop and think before we act. However, for children with ADHD, such natural abilities are beyond their grasp. They have problems with controlling their behavior, as well as paying attention.

The primary symptoms of ADHD are inattention, impulsiveness, and hyperactivity, which hinder one's ability to control behavior. ADHD children seem to have a "Who cares?" attitude, disregarding warnings about the consequences of their actions. It often seems as if their hasty behavior is based on what they are interested in at that moment, rather than considering the outcomes. Thus, ADHD children are considered to be impulsive.

ADHD is commonly described as a lack of self-control. Russell A. Barkley, Ph.D., an expert on ADHD, explains that this disorder involves an impairment in the ability of the individual to inhibit responses to situations or events.

If you believe that young children are the easiest group of people to diagnose with ADHD, think again. In reality, young children are actually the most difficult group to diagnose. Even normal young children commonly display varying degrees of inattention, impulsivity, and overactivity. It is difficult to distinguish when problems in these areas are due to the child's normal development or whether they are the result of a more chronic disorders. Rather than make an uncertain diagnosis, it is sometimes more prudent to wait and see how the young child with ADHD-like symptoms matures.

It is important to understand what ADHD is and how it looks in the young child for early detection of the disorder. Often, children with ADHD are not diagnosed until later in the elementary school years. By that time, they may have developed additional behavioral and social problems and may be perceived by others as having emotional difficulties, when. These complications could often be traced back to the underlying ADHD issues.

We should attempt to identify and treat children with ADHD as early as possible. However, even with early intervention, we cannot prevent the course of the disorder continuing for many years for most children that are diagnosed with ADHD. Many children do not outgrow ADHD, nor is there a cure for this chronic disorder. To treat children most effectively, a combined treatment approach is often necessary. This usually means behavioral training for parents and the child, family and individual counseling, educational accommodations, and if necessary, medication.

Not only will the ADHD child's inattention, hyperactivity, and impulsivity appear at school, but such behavior will also interfere with family life, peer interactions, and many other activities in which the child participates. Children with ADHD may also have associated learning disabilities, emotional difficulties, and social and family problems. These must also be recognized and treated.

To make this book a practical guide for parents and teachers, we present typical problems with ADHD behavior that occur at home, at school, and in other situations. We offer remedies to deal with them. Please refer to the illustrated scenarios in this book together with your child to help you and your child learn how to deal with problem behavior.

This book discusses effective tools that you can use to manage the young child with ADHD. The method of redirection, or re-focusing the child's behavior, is presented. Redirection can be a very effective tool for altering the child's behavior.

Another technique we will discuss is the use of imaginative play. As part of imaginative play, we expand upon something most young children are naturally comfortable with—creating a pretend friend who can help guide the child and help anchor positive internalized messages.

We also discuss behavior modification, the most popular and commonly employed method of managing behavior. However, it may not be as useful for all children since research indicates that behavior modification may not always manage impulsive behavior successfully.

Similarly, self-instruction (which is a form of behavior modification) is less effective with more severely afflicted children, who are highly impulsive. Nevertheless, for those children who may benefit from using problem-solving and calming strategies, we have included training in this area.

In addition, we review current assessment instruments and discuss the role they play in evaluating children for ADHD. Treatment methods including medications, counseling,, and diets are also discussed in detail. We have also prepared a Parent's Survival Guide, which features various authors' ideas and helpful hints to guide parents through the difficult times with their child.

Throughout this book, you will notice an emphasis on redirecting our own thinking to help our ADHD children redirect their behavior.

With this practical guidebook in hand, we are confident that you will be better equipped to deal with your feelings and effectively manage the behavior of your ADHD child.

Cathy L. Reimers, Ph.D.
Bruce A. Brunger

CHAPTER 1

A Day in the Life of
Young Children with ADHD

Joey:
The On-Again, Off-Again Child

It is 4:30 a.m. Joey, a 5-year-old, bounds out of bed and runs noisily to his parents bedroom as he does every morning. No matter how early or how late Joey went to bed the night before, he always wakes up at 4:30 a.m. Joey's parents, Alan and Lisa, often joke that they never need an alarm clock in the house. Alan and Lisa are still sleeping as Joey bursts through the door and pounces on their bed like a cannonball, trying to snuggle in between the twisted maze of blankets, sheets, arms, and legs. With his brown hair disheveled from tossing and turning in his own bed the previous night, Joey sports a mischievous, impish grin. Joey simply cannot lay still. He wiggles, giggles, pokes his parents in their ears, and does his best to wake them up.

Alan and Lisa, rudely awakened from their blissful sleep, try feebly to negotiate a peaceful truce with Joey, but it is no use. Joey isn't taking prisoners. The only way Joey is going to leave his parents' bedroom is together with them. Alan and Lisa will either trudge along half-awake to get Joey's breakfast ready, or storm after Joey to catch him and send him to the corner for waking them up so early.

Joey takes forever getting dressed before having his breakfast. He is always distracted by a toy, a bird singing outside his bedroom window, a spider on the wall, or any other little thing that draws his attention from the task at hand. After waiting in vain for nearly 15 minutes for Joey to get dressed, Alan and Lisa decide not to wait for him anymore and start breakfast without him.

Joey gets upset for being left out. He is certain they are eating some yummy pastry or other sweets without him. He starts whining and throws a tantrum, still in his underwear. Alan and Lisa try their best to ignore Joey's protests, but Joey escalates things by taking his sideshow from his bedroom to the dining table. At five years of age, Joey is already an expert at pushing his parents' buttons. In no time at all, Joey manages to frustrate his parents, spoiling breakfast for everyone. Alan can't take it any longer, and angrily marches Joey back to his room and orders him to get dressed. The classic power struggle begins, as it has every day since Joey could talk.

"No!" Joey screams, as Alan points to the clothes which Joey should have put on, now strewn all around the room. "I don't want to!" Alan can feel his temper boiling, but he tries to be firm. "Get dressed right now. I mean it!"

"Noooooo!" Joey shrieks back, sticking out his tongue at his father for added emphasis. Alan then orders Joey to go take some time out in the corner. Joey doesn't budge, still protesting. Alan has to pick him up off the floor, kicking, screaming, and scratching, and hauls Joey to the other side of the house to "the corner," plopping him down with an air of triumphant finality. In Alan's mind, he has won the contest, but Joey is far from feeling beaten. Alan turns his back to walk away and is blistered by a blood-curdling scream from Joey, who angrily protests being sent to the corner. Joey throws a pillow at his dad, kicks the walls, and blows loud raspberries at his father, derisively yelling after him, "I don't like you! Hah!"

Alan turns and walks toward Joey, not willing to be outdone. "All right young man, you asked for it. I'm adding 5 more minutes on the time-out clock for that!" Joey screams even louder, as Alan shuts the door on the tirade and returns red-faced to the breakfast table.

It has been the same routine, every morning, for the last two years.

Strangely enough, after "doing his time" in the corner, Joey emerges more calm, cool, and collected. He gets dressed, eats his breakfast almost without incident and gets ready to go to preschool with his mother.

Both father and son keep their distance from each other for the rest of the morning, both feeling that something is wrong, both feeling hurt, but unwilling to face each other. Joey quietly hops in the car with his mom, and heads for school, alone in his thoughts.

Arriving at the preschool, Joey hangs up his coat, and sits glumly in the circle with the rest of his classmates. The vacuous expression on his face catches the attention of his teacher, Ms. Reynoso, who cheerfully tries to involve Joey in the class discussion. Joey almost seems embarrassed by the attention from his teacher and classmates, and becomes less social at first, then relaxes, and later joins in with the songs and other circle activities.

Despite the rough start to his day at home, Joey has a good day at school. Joey's behavior seems like any other normal kid in class. He happily goes from one activity to another, hangs out with a couple of buddies and generally stays out of trouble. Any trace of the defiance and stubbornness he displayed at home is completely absent.

The only dark cloud in an otherwise sunny day at school is when Joey impulsively decides to demolish a classmate's tower, which is made of building blocks. He has no real reason for doing it, other than an urge to see how the blocks would fall. Joey's action starts a fight, which results in Joey being sent to take some time out in a chair. Again, Joey doesn't go quietly. He screams, kicks the chair, and throws it across the floor. Ms. Reynoso quietly responds by bringing the chair back and has Joey sit in it for a few minutes.

When Lisa comes to pick up Joey at the end of the school day, he bounces up to her, proudly waving some hastily-drawn, gloomy pictures that he made in class. "I had a good day at school today, Mommy!" says Joey, obviously pleased with himself. His pictures are all drawn in dismal colors, all featuring angry or sad-faced characters in fighting poses and he shows them off proudly. He is a chatterbox of excitement during the ride home, talking about his school day. However, Joey grows progressively quieter as they get closer to home.

Joey has a pleasant afternoon at home, playing nicely with his little brother and sister. When Alan arrives home later, Joey rushes up to him to proudly show his gloomy pictures. Alan tries not to show his disappointment at the pictures, and even helps Joey tape them up on the wall in his bedroom.

Alan is still feeling remorseful about the stand-off with Joey earlier that day. He tries to avoid anything that might turn into another argument or power struggle. Lisa tells Alan about Joey's good behavior throughout the day and reminds Alan to "catch Joey doing good." Alan smiles to himself and wonders how he can "catch Joey doing good" when he always seems to be getting into trouble.

At dinnertime, Joey starts to fidget. He touches his food with the back of his hand, sticks rice up his nose, and blows bubbles in his milk. Lisa and Alan make repeated requests for Joey to mind his table manners. Then Joey starts making silly noises at the table, rolling his eyes, sticking food out on his tongue, and lying down on his chair.

This sets Alan off again. "Joey, knock it off, will you? How many times do we have to tell you?" Joey is getting giddy at this point and won't settle down.

Alan has had enough. Without a word, Alan picks up Joey and marches to Joey's room. This time, Joey isn't screaming or yelling. He continues to make silly noises in his room while his parents finish dinner.

After dinner, the family settles down to watch a children's video together. Alan watches the TV, but his mind is elsewhere. He is anxious and agitated. After a while, Alan goes to the bathroom, closes the door, and looks hard at himself in the mirror. "My God, why is Joey always acting like this?" Alan says to himself as he puts on some shaving cream. "Why does everything have to be such a knock-down, drag-out power-struggle with that kid?"

And then, suddenly, everything breaks down.

Alan, usually a very self-controlled man, feels powerless as waves of anger and helplessness wash over him. His arms start to quiver, then his lips, then his knees weaken.

Shakily, he grabs hold of the edge of the bathroom sink, still fixing his stare into the mirror, eye-to-eye with himself. Tears pour down his face, streaming through the shaving cream.

Alan comes face-to-face with mixed emotions that he has repressed until now, a confirmation of something ugly and terrifying that has lurked in the back of his mind for the last three years: He doesn't like, indeed, almost hates, his son Joey.

Before he knows it, Alan hears himself sobbing, quietly at first, then it all gushes out–a deep, visceral cry that wracks his whole frame. His whole body shaking, Alan hangs his head over the bathroom sink. The shaving cream drips off his face into the basin, mixed with tears and great drops of sweat, as Alan's cries rip from his throat.

Alan's mind is racing. "My God, I hate Joey...I really HATE him! But why? He's my son! I shouldn't be feeling like this! But I can't take this anymore...why does everything have to be such a struggle with him? Why can't he just obey and be a good kid? God, I can't stand myself for feeling like this! What am I gonna do?"

Out in the living room, Lisa thought something terrible had happened when she heard Alan's first groan erupt from the bathroom. She ran over to the bathroom, and peeked inside, only to find her husband hunched over the sink, speechless. This is a side of Alan she has never seen in their 10 years of marriage and it frightens her.

"Are you all right, honey?" she asks nervously. Alan, shaking his head, can only muster a feeble wave to her, indicating that he wants to be left alone. By now, Joey, his four-year-old little brother, and 16-month-old little sister had run up to the bathroom door. "Mommy, why is daddy crying?" they ask innocently.

Embarrassed, Alan is still unable to talk through gushing tears. Lisa closes the door, scoots the children off to bed, and leaves Alan alone to exorcise his anguish. It takes Alan almost a half-hour to cry himself out.

Later, Alan and Lisa turn in for the night. Without a word, Lisa reaches over to give Alan a reassuring hug. However, Alan can only lay on his back, wide awake, staring helplessly at the ceiling, tired of the daily struggle, wondering how he could harbor such terrible feelings toward his son.

Ricky:
The Severely Afflicted Child

Joyce, a single mother, is awakened early one morning by a racket coming from the kitchen. "It must be Ricky. I wonder what he is into now." she says to herself, with a weary smile on her face.

She gathers her robe and feels around the pockets for a lighter and a cigarette as she makes her way to the kitchen. She almost dreads looking into the kitchen, wondering what new surprise awaits her. She finds Ricky, her four-year-old, sitting in the middle of the kitchen floor, happily engaged in a "cooking" project of his own making.

While his mother slept, Ricky had succeeded in climbing onto the kitchen counters, pulling out flour, sugar, baking soda, shortening and a bottle of vinegar from the cupboards, and was mixing them all together with some pretty green-colored dishwashing soap. Pots and pans were all over the floor, along with various cooking utensils. Ricky must have been at it for nearly a half hour. He was just about to plug in the hand-held beater when Joyce entered the kitchen.

Aghast at the sight, all that Joyce could blurt out was "Ricky!" Ricky paid no attention to his mother. He was too engrossed in his project. Joyce rushed over and yanked the electric beater from Ricky's sticky hands.

Joyce sighed at the mess. Ricky yelled for the return of the beater, tugging at his mom's robe, then kicked her shin. Joyce let out a curse at the pain in her leg and chased Ricky out of the kitchen. It was a typical start to another day with Ricky.

Joyce knew that something was wrong with Ricky ever since he was a baby. He never cuddled, didn't nurse well, and was always fidgeting, even in his sleep. As soon as Ricky could crawl, he was a nonstop motion machine. He graduated from crawling to running in no time at all, almost bypassing the walking stage. Joyce had to keep an eye on Ricky constantly, as he was very accident-prone. At 16 months, he got a hairline fracture in his leg from jumping off the couch, and managed to wiggle out of the leg cast three times during the first day.

Joyce first became suspicious that Ricky had ADHD when he was two years old. She was initially reluctant to seek counseling, but when Ricky was three years old, she went to see his pediatrician. The pediatrician suggested that Ricky be put on medication. However, Joyce felt very apprehensive using medications with Ricky. Joyce felt that putting him on drugs would be admitting that she had failed as a parent.

Ricky's ADHD behavior is worsened by a severe emotional disorder. Ricky is often unresponsive emotionally, doesn't hug, beats up his six-year-old sister, and often embarrasses Joyce in public. Even though Joyce tries hard to be a good parent to Ricky, she often feels drained by the end of each day.

Today was typical. Ricky was a disaster at school as well as at home. His way of saying "hello" to his classmates is by hitting them on the head or knocking them over. Needless to say, Ricky's behavior has not endeared him to his classmates, and he has no friends. No one interacts with Ricky in class, nor comes to his house to play. His voice has only two volumes, loud and louder. Ricky's emotional state vacillates unpredictably.   He is sweet and mellow one minute, and then angrily bounces off the walls the next. Joyce dreads picking him up at the end of each school day because she knows there will be an incident report a mile long from the teacher about Ricky's misbehavior. Joyce would love to enroll him in a special school where he can get more attention and care, but her limited income won't allow it.

The school has diagnosed Ricky as having a mild learning disability compounded with emotional problems. Not only does his learning disability pose a challenge for his teacher, but his incessant troublemaking often has the teacher chasing him around the classroom and frequently sending him to the time-out chair. The air of the classroom and the halls at school are frequently punctuated with the teacher's shrill voice: "Ricky! Don't do that!" "Ricky, stop!" "Ricky, come back here!"

Joyce decides to stop by the local supermarket for some grocery shopping on the way home from school. With Ricky and his older sister in tow, Joyce hurries through the parking lot and makes a beeline for the shopping carts.

She straps Ricky into the child seat, and has her daughter walks alongside the shopping cart. Joyce only needs to buy some milk and meat for tonight's dinner, so she expects to make a quick stop at the store. Once inside, Ricky cannot keep his hands to himself, and reaches for any package on the shelves. Joyce has to be constantly vigilant to ensure that he won't pull down some display or grab a package of cookies on the shelf. One time, Ricky managed to rip open a bag of M & Ms and scatter them all over the checkout counter.

Once home, Joyce can only hope to keep a faint semblance of order until Ricky goes to bed, usually at ten or eleven o'clock. Ricky is unusually agitated today. Something is bothering him, but he cannot articulate his feelings very well. At the dinner table, Joyce still uses a baby high chair to restrain Ricky during meals. He fights it, and tries to scamper out of the high chair, tipping the whole thing over and pulling the table cloth down in the process.

Food is spilled all over the shag carpet, and Ricky is both laughing and crying.

Ricky is barely out of the high chair when Joyce loses her composure. It has been a long hard day for Joyce, and she screams at the top of her lungs, "What is the matter with you?" Joyce bears down on him with a withering barrage of criticism. Ricky reacts and starts crying. Joyce starts crying, too.

Later that night, after Ricky is asleep, Joyce looks in on him before going to bed. She finds him sleeping with his back and legs up against the corner of the wall, almost standing on his head, frozen in a comical pose. His bed sheets are almost pulled off his bed, and his blanket is on the other side of the bedroom. Joyce gently rolls him back under the covers and then stands back to watch him sleep.

Joyce sometimes wishes that Ricky had never been born, and she hates herself for feeling that way about him. "If it weren't for that kid," Joyce mumbles to herself, "I would be able to enjoy trips to the mall, eat at restaurants, go to movies, and many other simple things that parents of "normal" children can do." But not her. It just didn't seem fair.

Joyce walks quietly back to her bedroom. Holding her head in her hands she throws herself on her bed and cries. How she wishes that there was someone to give her a hug and tell her that everything would be okay, that she's doing a great job being a parent to Ricky. But being single, there is no one there to give her a hug. All she can do is clutch a pillow.

Suzy:
The Spaced-Out Child

Little Suzy is almost 5 years old. Her father, George, is vice president of an architect firm and her mother, Lindsay, is an attorney who works at a child-advocacy organization.

Suzy is a gifted, bright child, but she keeps to herself and has no friends. Her classmates often ignore her, since she behaves so differently from the other kids. Suzy's teacher noticed how she wanders aimlessly around the room, not joining other children in any of the activities, apparently in a world all her own.

Suzy's parents have great expectations for her and they involve her in many community activities. They shuttle her from play groups to art classes and to soccer games. George and Lindsay are even thinking of enrolling her in a ballet or gymnastics class.

Lindsay senses that Suzy's behavior is different. She worries that Suzy has a problem of some sort and wants to seek professional help. George, on the other hand, is in complete denial about the reality of her problem. He thinks her unusual behavior is just a phase, and that Suzy will grow out of it. This difference of opinion has led to many an argument between George and Lindsay.

One Saturday morning, Suzy was playing in a pee-wee soccer match with her team, the "Pink Tornadoes." Her father attends every game and enjoys rooting for his little girl. Right in the middle of the game, during a most crucial play, Suzy starts to "space-out" while on the playing field. She suddenly turns from being a player, to being an onlooker. The ball zooms past her, and she doesn't make a move for it.

George is embarrassed, and yells from the sidelines, "Aw c'mon Suzy! You could've gotten that one!" But Suzy just stands there, absentmindedly staring off into the distance while the rest of the players run by her. Unable to contain himself, George bolts from the sidelines and runs over to Suzy. Grabbing her by the shoulders, George tries to shake her out of her daydream, yelling, "Why don't you get the ball? What's wrong with you, girl?"

Later at home, George recounts to Lindsay how Suzy spaced-out at the soccer game. Lindsay recognizes that George's pride won't allow him to recognize a problem with Suzy, and soon they get into an argument. After arguing for 30 minutes, Lindsay finally grabs George by the shoulders in frustration and screams at him, "Don't you get it, George? Suzy needs help!"

The Many Faces of ADHD

The stories of Joey, Ricky, and Suzy illustrate just a few of the many faces of ADHD and how this disorder can impact children differently. We shall revisit these three families at the end of this book to see how their lives have improved by putting the principles of this book into practice.

As the profiles of these families vividly illustrate, raising a child with ADHD is never easy. Parents have to make extra efforts to adjust their parenting styles, seek professional help, and make use of community resources as they raise their children.

Children with ADHD have needs like all other kids, but their poor self-control and low frustration tolerance often results in offensive, annoying, repulsive, or demanding behavior. This makes the job of parents and teachers challenging. Once you understand what ADHD is and how to deal with it properly, you will find that working with your child or student can be a deeply rewarding experience. In the next chapter, we will examine the nature of ADHD to better understand it.

CHAPTER 2

Understanding ADHD in the Young Child

What is Attention Deficit Hyperactivity Disorder (ADHD)?

Does your child have difficulty sitting still? Is your child easily distracted? Does your child shift from one uncompleted task to another? Does your child seem confused or in a fog? Is your child unable to work independently without supervision? Does your child have trouble paying attention or concentrating? These problems may be a result of ADHD.

ADHD is a developmental disorder of self-control. It is the most common mental health disorder diagnosed in children and affects up to 6 percent of children in the United States. Children diagnosed with this condition typically have problems with hyperactivity, impulsivity, or inattention. Sometimes all three areas are affected. Difficulties in these areas are to such an extreme that behavior and performance of these children is often impaired at home, in school, or in social and community settings.

Although for some children, ADHD symptoms diminish with time, the majority of children diagnosed will continue to have problems with hyperactivity, impulsivity, or inattention well into adolescence or even into their adult years.

Young children with ADHD, however, present interesting and unique challenges to parents and teachers. Those who are hyperactive and impulsive often exhibit significant behavioral problems. They have trouble following rules, playing cooperatively with other young children, and they are often difficult to manage. Those who are severely hyperactive wear out their care-givers through non-stop activity and unrelenting demands for attention. Many experts believe that ADHD can be identified by age two or three in children with severe hyperactivity or impulsivity. When ADHD is diagnosed early, parents can be better prepared to help their child succeed. This book focuses on the special characteristics of these young children.

If you are reading this book, you either have a child with ADHD in your family or your classroom. You may have blamed yourself for the child's problems or you may have been unfairly judged and criticized by others. Most parents of young children with behavioral problems are at a loss to deal with the daily stresses and challenges they face. To make matters worse, young children often have young mothers and fathers who may be inexperienced in child rearing. When faced with the challenges of a child with ADHD, their confidence is easily shattered.

Research shows that children with mild ADHD will display fewer and fewer episodes of ADHD behavior by the time they reach adulthood. However, children with more severe symptoms of ADHD may continue to have problems with inattention, impulsivity, or hyperactivity through adolescence and into their adult years. Early diagnosis and treatment is important to help prepare the child and the family for future challenges that could be faced.

The outcome statistics of ADHD are alarming. This is particularly true for those children who have significant behavior problems. For this group, surveys reveal that 30 to 50 percent may be held back a grade at least once in their school years. A substantial number of them may not complete high school. As many as half may have problems with social relationship. Up to 60 percent may show signs of seriously defiant behavior, leading to resentment of authority, fights with peers and siblings, and other behavior problems.

As a result of more frequent failure, criticism, and impulsive behavior, children with ADHD may be at greater risk for delinquency and substance abuse later in life.

To avoid grim statistics like these in the future, it is important that you start now, when your child is young, to recognize, understand, and find treatments for this condition. Early intervention and understanding may improve future outcomes for the child with ADHD.

Characteristics of ADHD in the Young Child

Young children with ADHD may have difficulty staying motivated to finish tasks. They may have difficulty delaying gratification. They may be more active than other children their age and may wander aimlessly from activity to activity. They may also have a difficult time comprehending and obeying rules.

They may not pick up on obvious social cues and they may have trouble making friends.

They may often not listen to directions, warnings, or scoldings. They may forget things easily and may seem absentminded. Their emotions are often intense, and they may be easily angered and frustrated. They may interpret words and expressions literally. They may often be bossy toward others. They may have trouble solving problems, and may lack self-control.

Parents and teachers easily notice inappropriate behavior in young children with ADHD, especially those who are hyperactive and impulsive. It is often useful to obtain a professional evaluation of the child's behavior and adaptive functioning to determine if a problem exists. Doctors and mental health professionals who evaluate ADHD children use special criteria to help them to make a diagnosis.

Diagnostic Criteria for ADHD

The fourth edition of the Diagnostic and Statistical Manual of Mental Disorders (DSM IV), published in 1994 by the American Psychiatric Association guides the health care professional in determining whether characteristics of ADHD are present in the child. The DSM IV provides a list of criteria to help professionals identify ADHD. The most current criteria are listed below:

1. Inattention. At least six of the following symptoms of inattention must have persisted for at least six months to a degree that is maladaptive and inconsistent with normal developmental levels:
   a. Often fails to give close attention to details or makes careless mistakes in schoolwork, work, or other activities.
   b. Often has difficulty sustaining attention in tasks or play activities.
   c. Often does not seem to listen to what is being said.
   d. Often does not follow through on

instructions and fails to finish schoolwork, chores, or duties in the work place (not due to oppositional behavior or due to failure to understand instructions).

e. Often has difficulties organizing tasks and activities.

f. Often avoids or strongly dislikes tasks (e.g., schoolwork or homework) that require sustained mental effort.

g. Often loses things necessary for tasks or activities.

h. Is often easily distracted by external stimuli.

i. Is often forgetful in daily activities.

2. Hyperactivity-Impulsivity. At least six of the following symptoms of hyperactivity-impulsivity must have persisted for at least six months to a degree that is maladaptive and inconsistent with normal developmental levels:

   HYPERACTIVITY

   a. Often fidgets with hands or feet, or squirms in seat.

   b. Leaves seat in classroom or in other situations in which remaining seated is expected.

   c. Often runs about or climbs excessively in situations where it is inappropriate.

   d. Often has difficulty playing or engaging quietly in leisure activities.

   e. Often talks excessively.

   f. Often acts as if "driven by a motor" and cannot remain still.

   IMPULSIVITY

   g. Often blurts out answers to questions before the questions have been completed.

   h. Often has difficulty waiting in lines or awaiting one's turn in games or group situations.

   i. Often interrupts or intrudes upon others.

3. The onset of symptoms must have occurred before seven years of age.

4. Symptoms must have been present in two or more situations (at home, at school, at work, etc.).

5. The disturbance must cause significant impairment or distress in social, academic, or occupational functioning.

6. Symptoms must not have occured during the course of a Pervasive Developmental Disorder, Schizophrenia, or other Psychotic Disorder, and are not better accounted for by a Mood Disorder, Anxiety Disorder, Dissociative Disorder, or Personality Disorder.

Three Types of ADHD

Depending on the symptoms exhibited, your child may have one of three types of ADHD as described in the DSM IV manual.

1. predominantly inattentive type;
2. predominantly hyperactive-impulsive type; or
3. combined type (exhibits symptoms of inattention and hyperactivity and impulsivity).

Children diagnosed with ADHD in preschool often have hyperactive-impulsive symptoms more than symptoms of inattention alone. Children with the predominantly inattentive type of ADHD are often identified later when their school work is affected by problems resulting from short attention span.

What Causes ADHD?

There is great interest in scientific circles about what causes ADHD. Most scientists agree that ADHD is a neurological disorder, which may be caused by differences in brain chemistry, brain activity, blood flow, or brain structure. The factors that may have caused such neurological differences in children with ADHD have been attributed to:

- Heredity
- Brain injury or abnormal brain development
- Exposure to toxic substances during fetal development (tobacco, alcohol, etc.)

Heredity is presumed to be the most common cause of ADHD. Much of our information about the inheritability of ADHD comes from family and twin studies. Researchers have discovered that ADHD tends to run in families. If a parent has ADHD, there is a better chance that one or more of their children will also have it. Several large studies of identical twins have provided additional evidence that ADHD is hereditary. If one identical twin has ADHD, there is a greater than 90 percent chance the other twin will also have ADHD.

Researchers generally agree that ADHD is *not* caused by the following factors:

- Sugar and chemical food additives
- Yeast
- Bad parenting or dysfunctional family life
- Allergies
- Fluorescent lighting
- Inner ear problems

There is still much to learn about ADHD and its causes. The information that is available, though incomplete, has helped us arrive at a better way to effectively manage ADHD than in previous years.

Learning Disabilities Associated with ADHD

Dr. Russell Barkley reports that between 20 and 30 percent of ADHD children have at least one type of learning disorder in math, reading, and spelling. Professionals describe a learning disability as a dysfunction in one or more steps in the learning process. These four steps are:

1. Input—how information enters the brain through the sense organs.
2. Integration—the processing and interpreting of the information.
3. Memory—storage of the information for later retrieval.
4. Output—sending out the information through muscle or language activity.

While speech and language problems may be apparent in preschool children with ADHD, more subtle learning disabilities may not be apparent until the child is in elementary school. It is important for parents and teachers to be aware that children with ADHD have a greater risk of learning disabilities than others.

Emotional and Behavioral Disorders

Many children with ADHD have long-standing problems with temperament and managing emotions. Sometimes the signs are noticeable from infancy. Parents may report that their ADHD children were irritable, temperamental, and demanding from birth. They had trouble with feeding and calming their child. Some children only slept for short periods of time. Sometimes, these problems of temperament and emotionality persist into childhood.

Many children with ADHD develop oppositional defiant disorder (ODD). They have a short fuse and quickly lose their temper. Hitting, fighting, and verbal attacks are common. Problems arise when they are asked to do something they do not want to do, or when they want to do something and you will not let them.

Other children with ADHD can develop anxiety, depression, and low self-esteem. They may deal with emotions by bottling them up. They feel nervous and upset. They become sad and have poor self-confidence. At times, parents and teachers unintentionally add to the child's emotional difficulties by being overly critical or by expecting more of the child than they should.

Some children with ADHD complain of headaches or stomachaches resulting from their anxiety. Other ADHD children cope with their frustration by controlling people and events around them. To avoid the pressures of class work, the ADHD child acts silly in class, often resulting in disciplinary action. Often ADHD children express their frustration and anxiety through open defiance of parents or teachers.

Social Problems

Children with ADHD often do not relate well to other children or adults. As a result, they may not fit in or be accepted. Being rejected by their peers can lead to feelings of loneliness, poor self-image, and low self-esteem.

A common problem for young children with ADHD is aggressive behavior. Due to poor impulse control, they may get into trouble for hitting, biting, etc. Some will try to boss others and act demanding. They control what play activity is done and how.

At school, the social problems of ADHD children are readily apparent in the classroom, hallways, and on the playground. They often do not pay attention to their teachers or classmates. They may interrupt the teacher or other students. Their fidgety behavior, noise making, and aggressiveness toward other children often cause others to dislike them.

Children learn about social rules in the preschool and early primary school years when they interact with others. This is especially challenging for the ADHD child, who does not pick up on the social cues to learn acceptable behavior. Unlike most children, the ADHD child has greater difficulty in sociability skills, such as taking turns, sharing, playing alone without bothering others, cooperative play with others, and engaging in imaginary play with others.

ADHD children typically have difficulty perceiving nonverbal cues in communication. They are at a disadvantage in recognizing facial expressions and interpreting gestures. They also have a hard time interpreting vocal cues in spoken language such as tone and emphasis.

Another social development characteristic often absent in ADHD children is their lack of social interest. Social interest means caring about others, having mutual respect, and being willing to cooperate with or serve others.

With such deficits, it is hardly surprising that the ADHD child is at a big social disadvantage. The ADHD child who cannot read nonverbal cues will be seen by others as rude, crude, and socially awkward.

Some special concerns about the social development of the ADHD child involve honesty, dealing with aggression, bedtime, and mealtime.

While most young children exaggerate and create stories, ADHD children often go a step further and make up lies. In general, children lie for the same reasons adults do. They want to get a good result or avoid a bad one. Young children, especially those impaired with ADHD, often do not see anything wrong with telling a lie to get what they want. If your ADHD child lies, try not to overreact. Tell him that it is important to tell the truth and that you are happy when he does so. At other times, you may simply choose to ignore his lying.

Parents and teachers of ADHD children often have to deal with the child's aggression toward others. When the ADHD child threatens other children, you need to understand the reasons for the behavior. It may be for power or control. It may also be an expression of frustration. It is important to help the child learn other productive ways of venting frustration or anger.

Mealtimes are often difficult for the parents of the ADHD child. Typical misbehaviors that occur at mealtime include playing with or spilling food, burping, fidgeting in the seat, talking, making noises, etc. Parents of children with ADHD are often reluctant to eat out at restaurants for fear of public embarrassment.

Bedtime is another challenge for the ADHD child. Like most young children, the ADHD child often resists going to bed on time. To avoid going to sleep, the child may make demands for a drink, a hug, a trip to the bathroom, or one more bedtime story. ADHD children typically find it difficult to wind down at the end of the day, especially if the day was filled with excitement.

In this chapter we discussed what ADHD is and some of the problems that accompany it. If a young child is diagnosed as having ADHD, possible emotional and social problems must also be identified and treated. In the next chapter we will provide you with tools to help you effectively address your child's ADHD and the associated problems.

CHAPTER 3

Building Self-Esteem and Improving Social Skills

Self-Esteem in the Young Child

Self-esteem is a favorable impression of oneself. It is a feeling of personal worth. We value ourselves when we have a positive self-image. When children feel valued, loved, and confident, they are better able to meet the challenges around them.

Early childhood is a critical period in which the seeds of self-esteem are planted. A young child's self-worth is influenced by the accomplishments they have and the way they perceive people's reactions to their behavior. In this chapter we will discuss how parents and teachers may build self-esteem in the young child.

Start with Respect

Mutual respect is the foundation on which to build the child's self-esteem. Parents need to show their children that they love and respect them. They should consider children's feelings and show respect by praising special qualities and talents. Give compliments. Discover the child's interests and support them. Allow the child to make his/her own choices when possible. Instead of criticizing, respectfully point out a child's strengths. For example:

"You drew such a great picture! Let's post it on the refrigerator!"

"You are so good at building blocks. Let's make a castle together."

"You really seem to like Winnie the Pooh, so why don't we get another Winnie the Pooh book at the store?"

"Would you like to eat hot dogs or spaghetti tonight?"

"Your cereal bowl got knocked over. Next time, you will try to be more careful with your elbows."

Encouragement is Essential

Encouragement that is focused on children's strengths help them develop positive attitudes about themselves. When children are encouraged, we show that we accept them for what they are, not for what they do. Encouragement does not expect perfection, but it recognizes effort and improvement. Through encouragement children may learn to appreciate their own special qualities.

How can you encourage your child? Parents and teachers can show appreciation for a child's efforts, improvements, strengths, and special qualities. A sense of humor is important because it shows the child how to deal with mistakes in a positive way.

The Language of Encouragement

In the book, *Parenting Young Children*, Don Dinkmeyer, Sr., Gary D. McKay, and James S. Dinkmeyer provide the following examples of encouraging phrases:
1. "You can do it."
2. "Thanks. That helped me a lot."
3. "I need your help on ____."
4. "You really worked hard on that!"
5. "How do you feel about it?"
6. "You're getting better at ____."

Social Skills Training

Young children who are hyperactive and impulsive often have serious problems with socialization. They may either lack social skills or may lack the ability to control their actions sufficiently to behave appropriately. The result is often either verbal or physical aggression, which inevitably leads to social rejection and isolation.

The goal of social skills training is to help the child learn and implement skills necessary to get along better with others. The training involves (1) explaining to the child what to do when social problems arise, (2) demonstrating the desired social behavior, and (3) having the child practice it. Thomas W. Phelan, Ph.D. describes some of the skills that children with ADHD often need to learn and practice. They include:
1. Following directions
2. Giving/receiving positive feedback
3. Sharing
4. Compromising
5. Dealing with name-calling or teasing
6. Sending an ignoring message
7. Joining a conversation
8. Problem solving
9. Saying "No" to stay out of trouble

Children with ADHD need practice to recognize and react positively to various social cues. They need to know that not only is it polite to pay attention to social cues, but it also helps them understand others' feelings.

It is important to rehearse proper social skills with your child at home so he or she will be better equipped for the daily interactions in the outside world. John F. Taylor, Ph.D., in his book, *Helping Your Hyperactive/Attention-Deficit Child*, provides a useful outline for parents who want to teach social skills to their children at home. He suggests that these parent-child training sessions at home be approximately 15 minutes long. Taylor's method consists of six steps, the first letters of which spell "SCORED."
1. **S**how. Act out the social skill.
2. **C**oach. Describe the skill in detail, explaining how it is helpful, its benefits, its importance, and the negative consequences of not using it.
3. **O**ffer self-reminders. Give the child self-reminding phrases for how and when to use the new skill.
4. **R**ehearse. Role play the skill in a realistic situation. Be sure to provide feedback on the child's performance. Practice with your child until he or she gains confidence and can respond automatically with the new skill. Scripts, cards, mirrors, and tape recorders can be helpful tools in the rehearsal.
5. **E**ncourage. Always provide positive reinforcement about the child's efforts and progress. Share in the joy as your child masters the skills.
6. **D**ebrief. Set a goal to have the child use the skill at least once a day. Review the child's progress at bedtime.

For example, children with ADHD anger easily when teased by other children. You want to teach them effective ways of dealing with teasing. Tell your child the exact words you want him to use in such a situation ("Stop teasing me!"). Then instruct him to walk away. Next, role play with him, with you posing as your child, and him posing as the bully. Then reverse the roles, coaching your child to use the same words without getting angry.

Practice until the child can respond with confidence. Review the benefits of this new skill with the child, and point out what could go wrong if it isn't used. Encourage the child daily, and tell him/her to report to you about success with using the new skill.

In addition to practicing at home, ADHD children can benefit greatly by joining a social skills training group. They can work on their skills with other children, under professional supervision.

Promoting Your Child's Social Development

"Nobody seems to like Billy. How can we help him to make friends?" Does that predicament sound familiar? I have counseled many worried parents and teachers about how to help ADHD children like Billy fit in socially with their peers.

Social development for an ADHD child is a rough road. As a parent, watching your little Billy being rejected by other kids his age can tear your heart out. It just doesn't seem fair sometimes. You know that Billy can be sweet, kind, caring, and fun. Why can't other kids see that in him? You work with Billy at home and help him cope, but when it comes to Billy making friends on his own, it seems hopeless. You see Billy's loneliness. You see his self-esteem plunge as he is rejected over and over by the other children. It often seems as if the only friend little Billy has in the world is you. You're the only one who seems to be on his side.

With their impulsivity and hyperactivity, it should come as no surprise that ADHD children have serious problems getting along with other kids their age. Other kids have a hard time interacting with someone who is impulsive, aggressive, blunt, frank, and easily upset. ADHD children typically end up with bad reputations or become the subject of many cruel remarks by other kids.

David Guevremont, Ph.D., an expert on social interaction problems, recommends that parents try the following:
1. Practice good social skills at home.
2. Arrange for positive peer contacts at home.
3. Set up positive peer contacts in the community.
4. Get help from the child's school.

To help your child work on social skills in the home, you could set up a point system using poker chips or stickers. Limit your training to one or two social behaviors, such as sharing, keeping hands to oneself, speaking quietly, staying in one's seat, not being bossy, or some other social behavior. Write them down on a chart that both you and your child can see. When your child is playing with other children, call the child over to you and quietly remind him about the new skills. Remind your child that he can earn points or poker chips for practicing the new skills and can lose points for unacceptable behavior. Catch your child behaving well, and reward him with a point or poker chip. Be sure to set time aside each day to review the new social skills. Perhaps do a short role play with him for practice.

One very helpful coaching technique is to videotape the child's interactions with playmates. Videotapes can help ADHD children observe their own behavior, since they are often unaware of how they act with others. Try to select several instances on the tape where the child is showing appropriate behavior and give lots of positive feedback. Then pick out one or two instances where the behavior was inappropriate and explain how it could be improved next time.

While you practice good social skills with your child at home, try to pay attention to possible problem areas such as:

- playing with another child or group;
- starting and maintaining a conversation with another child (including listening to the other child's words and feelings, and taking turns in the conversation);
- resolving conflicts; and
- sharing things with others.

Next, you should arrange for positive peer contacts at home for your child. This is sometimes difficulty, however, you could start by encouraging your child to invite classmates over to your home after school or on weekends. Call other parents and invite their child to come and play. Don't leave the time unstructured. Plan things for the children to do. Rent a video, do crafts together, and have structured playtime. Such structured peer contacts at your home can be the foundation for positive peer contacts that may foster friendships.

When other children are at your home to play, make sure their play doesn't escalate out of control. Look for signs like increasing silliness, horse play, or roughhousing, which may signal that things might get out of control. Intervene with snacks or a more calmer, structured activity to break up the momentum. You could talk with the kids to get their attention off of themselves and on to you, or take them to a different place to play.

Above all, you have to keep a tight lid on aggressive behavior at home. Watch your own behavior and that of family members. Whenever possible, do not let your child watch violent cartoons or other TV programs. Do not allow your child to invite home any aggressive playmates from school. The age of your child's playmates should not be a concern, as long as they display positive social behavior for your child.

If these activities are successful you may want to branch out into community-based activities. You can enroll your child in scouts, clubs, sports, hobby groups, or church social groups. Summer camps or day activity programs can also be beneficial. They all offer structured activities under adult supervision, which will keep your child's behavior from getting out of control. Group activities that require a great deal of cooperative effort or complex rules should be avoided. Avoid activities that require a lot of idle time. The goal is to keep your child busy. Also, try to avoid excessively competitive situations, which may only frustrate your child.

Whenever possible, try to involve your child in cooperative learning tasks with other children. Activities like building a model together, setting up a tent in the backyard, running simple science experiments, or doing an arts and crafts project will give opportunities for the kids to show positive feelings toward each other.

Finally, you can get help from your child's school to work on social skills. Meet often with your child's teacher to learn about your child's behavior in the classroom. You can encourage the teacher to try out some of the behavior modification methods you are using at home. You could ask the teacher to give special responsibilities to your child in front of the other children to help them see your child in a positive light. Together with your child's teacher you could also draw up a behavior chart or rating card which focuses on the skills your child is trying to master in class. Ask the teacher if the school is running any social skills workshops for children, and enroll your child in one. If necessary, consider whether your child needs to be placed on medication to help him control disruptive behavior in class.

As you help your child learn and practice new social skills, be realistic about your expectations for change and what you will be able to achieve. Look for opportunities to practice those new skills and avoid situations that will lead to failure and frustration. The more patiently you work at it, the better adjusted your child will be as he interacts with peers.

CHAPTER 4

Communication with Your Child

Effective Communication

Communication between parents and their children is a key to healthy emotional and behavioral adjustment. Effective communication is particularly important when raising a child with special needs such as ADHD. Take a moment to consider how you and your child talk to one another. As a parent, do you find yourself using words that hurt, put the child on the defensive, or pass judgments? Are you quick to interrupt your child or turn away when he is trying to tell you something. Are you apt to lecture, scold, or demand too much? Investigators visiting the homes of children with ADHD found parents to be more negative, demanding, and judgemental when they communicated with their child than parents of non-ADHD children. This is probably because these children are challenging and demanding on the parents who may become worn out and impatient.

Given the nature of children with ADHD, effective communication with your child may not be an easy task. Your goal should be to express yourself appropriately and to model good communication skills for your child to follow.

You could start by replacing negative words and phrases with positive ones. Think of any negative words or phrases you use around your child and practice positive alternatives. You could create a list of words and phrases and hang it on the wall to visually remind you each day. You can tape record your conversations with your child for instant playback and review.

On the following page is a list of common negative phrases that parents use with children, with more positive alternatives that you can practice.

You will notice a common characteristic of the positive phrases—they are not judgmental, insulting, or accusatory. One very effective way to communicate feelings without a judgmental tone is with "I-messages," based upon the *Systematic Training for Effective Parenting (STEP)* program. With "I-messages," you don't label or blame your child, you are telling him how you feel. To use "I-messages," simply follow these three rules:

1. State what behavior led to your feeling, (e.g., "When I see you leave your toys on the floor...").
2. State what you are feeling, (e.g., "I feel upset...").
3. Explain the consequences of the behavior, (e.g., "...because we may accidentally step on them and break them.").

Instead of saying this.....	Try saying this...
• Why did you do such a stupid thing?	• Tell me why you did that.
• Be quiet! Can't you see we're talking?	• Please don't interrupt.
• How many times do I have to tell you?	• Please listen carefully.
• Why can't you find something to do?	• Are you bored?
• You're always getting into trouble!	• Do you need help?
• I can't believe you did that!	• That's unacceptable.
• I'm warning you....	• Please listen to me.
• (Angrily) Knock it off!	• I need you to stop what you're doing.
• (Screaming) Stop being noisy!	• (Calmly) Use your inside voice, please.
• Stop running around like a maniac!	• Let's walk safely.
• You're really going to get it!	• I need you to follow the rules.
• You liar! I saw you do it!	• I want you to tell me the truth.
• Why are you fighting all the time?	• Fighting only hurts you and others.
• Why don't you do what I tell you?	• Do you understand what I asked?
• Can't you sit still?	• You need to stay in your seat.
• I've had it with you!	• I'm not happy with your behavior.

It is vitally important to maintain self-control when communicating, especially when your child needs to be corrected and disciplined. Angry actions on your part will most likely beget angry reactions from your child. Try to communicate your discipline calmly, decisively, and consistently.

For example, suppose you are driving in the car and your child takes off her seat belt and is jumping around in her seat. She refuses to calm down and put the seat belt on, even after repeated requests to do so. Pull the car over at a safe location. Instead of yelling at the child, calmly and firmly tell the child to get out of the car to take a time-out on the sidewalk with you. During the time-out, talk with your child using I-messages, such as, "I feel scared when you don't have your seatbelt on because you could get hurt if we have an accident." Or "I can't drive safely when you are jumping up and down in the car."

Be careful not to engage in too much conversation when correcting misbehvior as your actions will usually have greater impact than your words.

How to Communicate Your Love

You need to let your child know that you love her. A parent's love is very important in promoting positive self-esteem. Being supportive and giving respect to our children are two ways we can express that we love them, but there are other ways to tell them.

You could start by simply saying "I love you" each day. You can get creative and say it in several ways: "I love you THIS many tickles..." (then count off several tickles), or "Do you know how many people love you? (While counting on the child's fingers) There's Mommy, Daddy, Sister Lisa, Aunt Flo, Grandma Johnson...."

You can show your appreciation to your child in ways that say, "I love you." For example: "Good night Joey, I sure had fun with you today! I'm looking forward to seeing you tomorrow morning!" or "Tammy, you're such a great hugger! It's so much fun hugging you!"

You can express your love with touch as well as words. You can caress your child's hair while you sit on the couch watching TV, or hold hands when walking together, give a pat on the back, a nice hug as you tuck your child into bed at night, etc. For those ADHD kids who are not into soft touch, you can play "tag" with them or engage in a little rough-and-tumble play. Some kids enjoy being held upside-down. You can bounce your child on your knee, roll together on the floor—anything that brings you into contact your child and says non-verbally, "I love being with you."

You can take special time, one-on-one, with your child. During this time, give your full undivided attention to the child and enjoy an activity together. It is important to give this special time on a regular basis. When your child sees that you are taking time to spend with her, she will feel important.

And remember, when your child misbehaves, don't go overboard and launch into a tirade. What we say and do when our children misbehave is very important to their self-esteem and sense of being loved.

Finally, remember that for you to effectively communicate your love to your ADHD child, you must first come to grips with your own feelings. How do you really feel about yourself and about your relationship with your child? Take stock of your range of feelings and find out if there are any emotions getting in the way of expressing love to your child. Write up a list of those feelings. A typical list may include:

- Confused
- Overwhelmed
- Anxious
- Frustrated
- Impatient
- Misunderstood
- Angry
- Tense
- Stressed-out
- Embarrassed
- Disorganized
- Tired

Likewise, you could also make a simple list of feelings for your child, perhaps with illustrative pictures depicting each feeling. Your child can circle the pictures and show them to you. Such a list will contribute greatly to an exchange of feelings and understanding between you and your child. A sampling of feelings that you could review with your child could include:

- Wiggly
- Picked on
- Dumb
- Angry
- Can't wait
- Smart
- Friendly
- Forgetful
- Confused
- Special
- Scared
- Funny
- Happy
- Lonely
- Bored
- Teased
- Sad
- Unfair
- Hurt
- Hate
- Sorry
- Worried
- Left out
- Proud
- Excited
- Want to give up
- Good
- Feel loved

Effective and Reflective Listening

Expressing one's feelings and expectations verbally is only half of the communication process. The other half is listening. By listening carefully, we can help our children recognize, understand, and deal with their feelings. Reflective listening is a technique used in the *STEP* program, in which you reflect the feelings your child is expressing. This helps the child feel understood. It also helps him to verbalize his feelings more clearly.

Reflective listening follows three simple steps. First, establish eye contact with the child, at the child's eye-level, giving him your undivided attention. Second, ask yourself what the child is feeling, and think of a word that describes that feeling. Third, use that word as you talk with the child. The basic model looks like this:

You feel *(state the feeling)* because *(state the reason behind the feeling)*.

- You feel *angry* because *Susan took your doll.*
- You feel *excited* because *we're having company.*
- You feel *sad* because *you broke your toy.*
- You feel *happy* because *you painted such a nice picture.*

I-messages and reflective listening help you communicate more meaningfully with your child. While they do not ensure better behavior in your child, they can play an important role in shaping behavior in many situations.

CHAPTER 5

Effective Techniques to Manage Behavior

A Tool Bag of Techniques

Children with ADHD present enormous discipline challenges to parents and teachers. In this chapter we will present several effective tools which you can use singly or in any combination to immediately modify problem behavior. These tools are redirection, imaginative play, behavior modification, and self-instruction.

Behavioral Tools Help "Ease Off The Gas Pedal"

Why do these tools work? These behavior management tools provide structure and consistency to help the child regulate his own behavior.

As we mentioned earlier, try not to overreact to your child's problem behavior. You are only "throwing gasoline on the fire" because you are adding more stimulation to the child's already overstimulated emotions. When using these behavioral tools, it is essential that you react calmly, unemotionally, and logically so that the child can calm down. In this way, you can help the child "ease off the gas pedal," and thereby achieve more success in self-control.

A New Direction: Redirection

If you read *Jurassic Park* or saw the movie, you may recall the words of the chaos theory mathematician, Dr. Malcom. He sarcastically wondered what the scientists of Jurassic Park had done in bringing dinosaurs back from extinction. He explained "Your scientists were so preoccupied with whether or not they could, they didn't stop to think if they should."

This describes the dilemma of the child with ADHD who often acts before thinking. Similarly, parents and teachers also need to stop and think. We must redirect our thinking about the reasons behind the child's behavior and how to deal with a problem situation.

"Redirection" is one of the most common behavioral intervention techniques used to alter behavior. It is especially helpful with young children. Redirection is basically distracting the child by interrupting the current behavior and then quickly suggesting another activity, thereby moving the child into the suggested activity.

For example, if your daughter was crying, you could distract her with her favorite doll or toy. If your son is getting into the china cabinet, you could point out a bird in the back yard through a window. If you sense that your child is going to have a temper tantrum, you could pretend that there is a swarm of imaginary bees in the room. Then you could playfully suggest to the child to run with you into the next room. Once you are there, you could get him or her interested in another activity.

Another method of distracting the child is by getting the child's attention indirectly. For example, when your child is having a temper tantrum, do not say anything. Instead go into another room and start playing rambunctiously with some toys. The child will hear you playing, stop crying, and come to you to join the fun.

Imaginative Play

Another tool that parents and teachers can use is imaginary or pretend play. Three to five year olds are at their peak of imaginative play. Young children are naturally imaginative. Pretend play can be a very effective channel for their energy and emotions and can enhance their creativity. The use of a prop, such as a toy, in the role of a pretend friend may help the child to elaborate on and extend the pretend play. The play is extended as the child manipulates the object, reacts to it, and continues playing. Encouraging your child to create an imaginary friend relieves the loneliness and despair that he or she may feel, and provides someone else to share in the punishments that result from inappropriate actions. An imaginary friend can provide the child with both encouragement and comfort.

Dr. Marilyn Segal, Ph.D., the Director of The Family Center at Nova Southeastern University in Fort Lauderdale, Florida, is a developmental psychologist specializing in early childhood. She has studied and written extensively about the role of imaginary play.

She observed that one of the reasons why children pretend is to make sense of the world around them. As children play and replay familiar events, they understand them better. As children become familiar with a specific imaginary theme, they begin to recognize the difference between reality and fantasy.

Dr. Segal points out that another reason for imaginative play is that it provides children with emotional support to compensate for feelings of inadequacy. Children can act out scary events until their fears are under control. Imagination can also deflect feelings of loneliness and insecurity. A child could have a favorite doll, stuffed animal, or security blanket that help keep the child company in new or strange situations. Pretending can meet some of a child's social needs and can compensate for a child's lack of control over other events in the real world. Most of the time, rules are imposed on the child, such as when to get up, when to sleep, where to go to the bathroom, etc. In imaginative play, the child gets to set the rules, boss the characters around, and control the outcome.

An imaginary playmate or pretend friend can be particularly beneficial to a child who has special needs and challenges. A pretend friend can help the child unload some heavy emotional baggage and feel better about herself. By providing a pretend friend or confidant for the child, some of the child's anger can be displaced. Together, the child and pretend friend can share the responsibility for the child's actions and yet be supportive of each other as the child faces the consequences. Such a pretend friend can act as a good role model by providing guidance and encouragement.

What are some ways of fostering imaginative play? In her research, Dr. Segal studied families who were successful at imaginary play and found that there were two characteristics common in these families—the adults had special interest and talent for playing imaginatively with their children and a variety of materials or props were made available to the children.

The role of the adult is essential to the success of fostering imaginative play in young children. Dr. Segal notes that, for the youngster, the greatest inducement for pretending is to play with an adult or older child who enjoys it.

Some parents prefer to be actors, participating in a direct way in their child's pretend themes. Other parents are director-types, who gather props, suggest dialogue, draw pictures, or tell stories. There are also parents who prefer to be "appreciative audiences," who love to watch their children's pretend activities but do not participate often.

Whether or not parents are direct participants in an imaginative episode, they play a key role in helping their children find appropriate props. Some parents assemble common items around the house for the child's use. Other parents create the props.

Dr. Segal developed two types of lists to facilitate prop gathering for imaginative play. The first list includes props that are most conducive to actor-type play. These props correspond with the different ways children may choose to act out a role.

THINGS TO PUT ON
- Hats of all kinds
- Makeup and felt tip markers
- Belts, ties, bracelets, watches
- Grownup shoes, old clothes

PLACES TO GO TO
- Large boxes
- Blankets or sheets to make tents
- Porches

THINGS TO CARRY
- Pocketbooks and billfolds
- Lunch boxes
- Shopping bags
- Suitcases and briefcases

THINGS TO USE
- Toy telephone
- Keys

- Small notebook and pencil
- Bits of string and ribbons
- Dolls, puppets, stuffed animals
- Real or toy pots and pans
- Old typewriter or cash register
- Small boxes or containers

The second list includes props that especially encourage producer-director type play, where children can set up playscapes.

READY-MADE PLAYSCAPES
- Playhouses, doll houses
- Toy villages and farms
- Toy railroads

MINIATURE TYPE PROPS
- Small cars, trucks, and planes
- Small plastic animals
- Plastic TV characters
- Fisher-Price® people

RAW MATERIALS
- Boxes and baskets
- Chalkboard and chalk
- Squares of fabric, linoleum, or rugs
- Flannel board or colorform sets
- Wood or plastic blocks
- A heavy tag board or plywood square to use as a roof or floor
- Crayons, water colors, and paper

Equipping your home with such props will open up a whole new world of imagination and creativity for your child. Props will allow you as a parent to help redirect your child's behavior toward positive imaginary play.

However, Dr. Segal makes an important point about pretend play. Even with all the ingredients for pretend play, it cannot flower without a foundation of real world experience. The more meaningful experiences children have, the greater their potential for play. Some parents fill their children's rooms with toys, feeling secure in the thought that they are contributing to their children's development. But Dr. Segal explains that a toy is a replication of a real world thing, and if a child has not experienced it in the real world, he or she will have difficulty with the analogy and cannot use the toy in pretend play. Most of the important experiences for young children are the everyday routine events, such as getting dressed, eating, cleaning up, going to the grocery store, taking a bath, etc. Other experiences could be a trip to the zoo or museum, an airplane ride, or a Thanksgiving dinner. Still other important experiences come from TV or books. Parents need to choose toys and props carefully to reflect the real world experiences of their children to help them maximize imaginary play. Properly nurtured imaginary play will be a greatly effective tool to help manage your child's behavior.

Behavior Modification

Another behavior management tool is behavior modification. This is based on the idea that a child can <u>learn</u> to exhibit appropriate behavior while inappropriate behavior can be reduced or eliminated.

The key to effective behavior modification is collaboration and consistency. Parents need to develop a plan together, agree on it, and stick to it. Often parents will work on teaching a specific behavior at home and will ask the child's teacher to help the child learn and practice similar behavior at school. Teachers and parents must work together to maintain the plan's momentum during the time the child is at school. Daily report cards about the behavior from teacher to parent can be a great help in maintaining such consistency.

Research on parent and teacher management of the behavior of children with ADHD clearly indicates that both positive and puni-

tive measures, often in combination, work best in disciplining children. Young children require heavy doses of positive reinforcement and encouragement. If you ever hope to change your child's behavior, remember that rewarding desired behavior is far more effective than punishment alone. Certainly, there will be many times when you will have to discipline the child for misbehavior. But the emphasis (and most of your attention) should be on the positive side. Reward or praise him or her for choosing the right behavior.

Using Positive Reinforcement

When thoughtfully applied, positive consequences can have a dramatic effect on the behavior of the child. When positive consequences are immediate and frequent, the child will probably perform better in school as well.

You need to determine what positive consequences will actually strengthen a desired behavior. Observe the child's actions, and you will be able to identify consequences that would be reinforcing for the child. If you are a teacher, it is also important to talk with the child's parents to gain further insights.

In their book, *Meeting the ADD Challenge: A Practical Guide for Teachers*, Steven Gordon and Michael Asher provide the following list, which provide some positive reinforcers you can use at home and at school:

EFFECTIVE REINFORCERS AT HOME

1. Social Reinforcers
   - Hugs
   - Pats on the back
   - Verbal praise
   - High fives
   - Kisses

2. Privileges or Activities
   - Dressing up in adult clothing
   - Having a late bedtime
   - Taking a trip to the park
   - Playing on the swing set

- Helping make dessert
- Going to the movies
- Playing with friends
- Spending the night with friends
- Feeding baby
- Listening to the stereo
- Reading a special bedtime story
- Going to a ball game
- Making a home video
- Eating out
- Choosing a menu for a meal
- Baking something
- Going somewhere alone with a parent
- Planting a garden
- Planning a day's activities together
- Using tools to make something
- Choosing a TV program
- Going fishing
- Being excused from chores
- Camping out in the backyard

3. Material Reinforcers
   - Toys
   - Snacks
   - Books
   - Clothing
   - Pets

4. Token Reinforcers
   - Money
   - Stars on a chart
   - Own bank account
   - Allowance
   - Poker chips to exchange for favors or gifts

EFFECTIVE REINFORCERS AT SCHOOL

- Having extra or longer recess
- Helping the custodian
- Being group leader

- Fixing the bulletin board
- Going to the school library
- Running errands
- Listening to records/tapes
- Being hall monitor
- Playing a game
- Sharpening pencils
- Helping the librarian
- Partying
- Having choice of a seat mate
- Having free time
- Story time
- Playing an instrument
- Having lunch with teacher
- Having snacks
- Erasing the chalkboards
- Tutor another student
- Getting stars
- Getting special certificate
- Wearing a special badge
- Happy face on paper
- Demonstrate a hobby to class
- Being cafeteria helper
- Free activity time

Reinforcements can be classified by type:
- biological
- symbolic
- activity
- social
- self- reinforcers

Biological reinforcement is food and drink. Special foods or beverages can be used as rewards for positive behavior.

Symbolic reinforcement consists of stars, stickers, points, tokens, etc. They are used as a means of exchange for desired objects and activities. For young children, stars, stickers, etc. have a reinforcement value of their own.

Activity reinforcers are special events, such as being allowed to help make cookies, going to the park, etc.

Social reinforcement consists of the parent or teacher giving attention and praise.

Self-reinforcement is ultimately what we want to motivate the child. Self-reinforcement consists of the child giving himself/herself a positive consequence for a job well-done. It can range from simply praising oneself to enjoying personal satisfaction from the performing the act. Self-reinforcement builds self-esteem, which helps motivate children to achieve.

Different Types of Punishment

Reprimands. The flip side of positive reinforcement is punishment. Verbal reprimands can be a form of punishment. Prudent reprimands are more effective than imprudent reprimands. The difference is that prudent reprimands are simple statements referring to the adult's displeasure with a particular behavior. Imprudent reprimands also convey displeasure, but are often accompanied by unnecessary lectures, emotionality, threats, etc.

Response Cost. Another type of punishment that is often used successfully with children who have ADHD is called "response cost." This involves assessing a cost for misbehavior. In some cases, the cost may be the loss of a privilege or loss of points or tokens. The main emphasis with this type of punishment is on reducing or eliminating negative behavior. It is often useful to pair a response cost system with a positive reinforcement system to reward appropriate behavior at the same time.

Time-Out. Boredom punishments can also be quite effective, especially with young children. These consist of time-outs. In "sit and watch" time-outs, the child must sit and quietly observe the rest of the class or family enjoying an activity. During "sit and think" time-outs, the child is sent away from the rest of the family or class to think about his/her misbehavior.

Over-Correction. Another form of punishment requires some effort from the child. If a child is messing up a room, have him/her stop and put everything back in its proper place. Another technique would be to require the child not only to put everything back in its proper place, but also spend additional time to clean the room even more.

Positive Practice. Another effective variation is having the child repeat the positive practice over and over. For example, if a child tends to drop litter on the floor, you have the child pick up the item, bring it to the wastebasket, and put it in. Then have the child take the item out of the wastepaper basket again, walk back to where he/she dropped it on the floor, and repeat the process of bringing it to the wastepaper basket, repeating this process several times. The child quickly dislikes having to repeat the action over and over, yet it requires the child to practice the desired behavior.

Remember that young children, and particularly those with ADHD, often respond to rewards and punishments differently than older children. Long-term rewards are less meaningful to the young child who cannot wait that long. Young children are more likely to be motivated if rewards are immediate. If given the choice, they will choose a smaller, immediate reward over a much larger, delayed reward. Rewards for ADHD children must usually be of a greater significance, providing greater stimulation. Also, some rewards that worked at first may lose their appeal over time, and new rewards may have to be substituted to sustain the child's motivation.

Likewise, punishments that are not immediate are soon "out of sight, out of mind" with young children. Some children seem insensitive to or less responsive to scoldings and time-outs. Such methods only work in the short-term anyway. Thus, for achieving long-term results, an individualized use of both positive and negative consequences will be far more successful.

Whenever consequences are used, the following guidelines given by Gordon and Asher can help ensure success:

1. Immediate feedback for the child's good and bad behavior.
2. Consequences must be delivered more frequently.
3. Incentives must be more substantial and more attractive, and rotated frequently. Positive consequences must always be tried before negative consequences. Also, negative consequences must never be used by themselves: always use them in connection with appropriate positive consequences.

As you get started on your behavior modification plan, you as parents must be the ultimate authority on the house rules with your child. You make the rules. Your decisions are final. Do not get sucked into reasoning, bargaining, threatening, arguing or debating the rules with your child. If you do, you lose. Make it clear to the child that the rules must be obeyed.

Before you make your behavioral plan for your child, identify which behaviors need modifying. Observe your child, and write down what led to the misbehavior, what the misbehavior was, and the consequence of that behavior. You might end up with a long list of behaviors, but often you can categorize them into a few major areas.

Dr. Larry Silver notes that unacceptable behaviors often fit one of three basic categories:
1. Physical (hitting, hurting others, damaging property, etc.)
2. Verbal (yelling, teasing, using bad words, threatening, etc.)
3. Noncompliance (not listening/doing what was asked, defiance, etc.)

It is a good idea to look for relationships between the misbehaviors and the events that preceded them. You might discover, for example, that Jenny tends to misbehave when she's catching a cold or when she's feeling tired or hungry. Or, you might observe that Jenny tends to misbehave after coming home from school or when she is off her medication. Sometimes her misbehavior seems to be linked to a learning disability.

Once you know the areas your child needs to improve, you can set up your initial plan. List a few behaviors you want to work on first, and devise a consequence that you can easily implement on a consistent basis. Also decide what rewards you will give for good behavior. It is important to have pre-planned responses. Also, if there are any siblings, include them in the plan, too.

Next, make a chart and divide each day into parts. A sample behavior modification chart is given in the appendix for your reference. The purpose of the chart is to help the child identify and practice good behaviors. The chart is not meant to be a record of misbehaviors. You check off or place stickers for the periods when the child has demonstrated good behavior.

Rewards can be provided on a daily basis and a special reward can be given at the end of the week. When determining what the rewards should be, seek your child's input. You have the final decision, of course, but allowing your child to suggest what kinds of rewards he/she would like would help enlist his/her cooperation in the plan.

Affection and encouragement as daily rewards are usually better than giving material ones. Such daily rewards could include doing something special with a parent, being able to stay up late for an agreed amount of time, etc. The end-of-the-week rewards are usually given when the child has met his or her goal of earning a certain number of points. Such weekly rewards could include going to a movie, eating out, having a friend sleep over, etc. You can write these rewards on the chart as a reminder to yourself and your child.

Now that you have the rewards figured out, what about the consequences for misbehavior?

Effective behavior management, particularly for the hyperactive-impulsive child with ADHD, requires a combination of reinforcement and consequences. Time-outs are universally recommended as the most appropriate means of dealing with unacceptable behavior.

Why? Time-outs give you and your child a chance to calm down and get the behavior under control. Time-out is an opportunity for reflection about the misbehavior. It is an easy and unemotional way of correcting misbehavior. If used consistently, time-outs will train your child to stop and think first, rather than act impulsively.

When your child misbehaves, he/she is removed from the area and told to sit quietly in a corner or another room for a brief period of time (often using a timer). This gives you and your child a chance to cool off. When the time is up, he/she is given the opportunity to start over without further scolding. For more details and pointers on how to use time-outs effectively, please refer to the Time-Out Guidelines in Appendix C.

Linking rewards and time-outs will work, if you are consistent. Your child will test you at times, so be persistent! Your child must know the rules and behave accordingly. The ultimate goal of any discipline program is to guide the child to be responsible and cooperative. Explaining appropriate behavior to young children and modeling such behavior in yourself is extremely important.

If parents rely on rewards too much, their children will only be motivated by the rewards themselves. Likewise, presenting consequences as punishments only teaches the child to be angry and bases the relationship on fear. Over punishing a child by yelling, threatening, or spanking can damage self-esteem, can cause a child to be afraid of parents, and can often foster a spirit of rebellion.

There are many methods you can use to discipline your child effectively. Authors Don Dinkmeyer, Sr., Gary D. MacKay, and James S. Dinkmeyer present several methods using the word "DISCIPLINE."

D   Distracting the child, then steering her toward acceptable behavior

I   Ignoring misbehavior when appropriate

S   Structuring the child's environment

C   Controlling the situation, not the child

I   Involving the child through choices and consequences

P   Planning time for attention and loving

L   Letting go to allow the child to act on her own

I   Increasing your consistency

N   Noticing positive behavior

E   Excluding the child with a time-out

At its heart, discipline is not punishment; it is teaching. Teaching should always be done in a helpful, respectful way.

Once you have everything running smoothly, you can build on your success and move on to the second step of your plan–helping your child to understand the difference between acceptable and unacceptable behavior. One good way to do this is by talking about the incident with your child.

These discussions should happen after the child is disciplined. It could be at the child's bedside at the end of the day, or in a quiet room at some time after the incident. Discuss what happened, without sounding critical or judgmental. Ask the child what he/she thinks he/she could do to stop it from happening again. Let your child talk. It's important not only to talk about what went wrong, but to help your child find other solutions.

As you learn the patterns of your child's behavior, and what events led to unacceptable behavior, you can coach your child to stop and think. An example: "Kenny, remember how we learned that if you grab things from others without asking, they will get angry at you? Do you remember what we talked about yester-day? Can you do something differently?"

Self-Instruction

Another tool to manage children's behavior is self-instruction. The goal of self-instruction is to train children to stop and think before they act. We teach children to think about the following five steps in problem solving.

1. Stop! What's the problem?
2. What are some plans?
3. What is the best plan?
4. Do the plan.
5. Did the plan work?

In general, it is difficult for children to stop and think about these problem solving steps, especially if they are impulsive. For the young child, the challenge is that much greater as their language skills are less sophisticated. Parents and teachers have to take a more active coaching role and use visual aids (e.g., a stop sign, posters with the steps written out, etc.) to help the child remember the process.

An imaginary playmate can be very useful when teaching a young child the five problem solving steps. The child can be taught to calm down by talking with her imaginary friend. Reasonable strategies or a plan can be devised for the child to follow. She can be taught to monitor her own behavior, which may help her control impulsive tendencies. This process could improve the chances for future academic and social success. Here is an example of how the child's imaginary friend can be incorporated into each of the five steps:

1. The parent or teacher tells the child that the imaginary friend is asking the child to stop and identify the problem.
2. The imaginary friend "tells" the child what the options are for the situation.
3. The imaginary friend helps the child

select the best option.
4. The child can then act appropriately, following the lead of the imaginary friend.
5. The parent/teacher, the child, and the imaginary friend meet together afterward to talk about how successfully the child handled the situation.

In addition to the problem-solving component of self-instruction training, parents and teachers can help the child learn to stay calm by teaching relaxation techniques. The child can be taught to identify physical signs of tension (loud voice, angry feelings, crying, etc). The child can be instructed to move away from the situation and relax. Some helpful relaxation strategies could include: visual imagery, breathing, and stretching exercises.

Visual imagery training can be done by having the child close his eyes, while you describe a soothing scene, such as floating on a cloud. Parents can practice this technique with the child at bedtime, rubbing the child's back while he rests in bed with his eyes closed. You can actually have the child do his own narrating out loud. The final step is for the child to be able to envision relaxing scenarios so that just the reminder of the word (like "cloud") can help him start his own calming visual imagery.

You can also train the child to use simple stretching, jogging in place, and deep breathing exercises to release tension. These can be practiced at home or at school.

Other safe ways to release tension or anger include writing down the angry feelings, scribbling on paper, tearing a piece of paper into tiny pieces (and cleaning up afterwards), pounding some clay, or hitting a punching bag.

CHAPTER 6

Typical Problems and Remedies

How to Use the Information in This Chapter

This chapter is one that you will refer to often. It is the parent's and teacher's guide to the cartoon scenarios contained in *The Buzz & Pixie Activity Coloring Book*. We have illustrated and described more than 75 common behavior problems that occur with young children at home, in school, and in other situations. The specific difficulties that children with ADHD have in these situations is described in the first illustration of each situation (Dr. Reimers Explains). The second illustration shows a postive outcome with an explanation (Dr. Reimers' Remedies) of how parents and teachers could respond to the misbehavior to create a positive result.

Buzz and Pixie are two children with ADHD. The adventures of Buzz and Pixie depict behaviors that typically occur with children in the home, at school, and in other settings. Each scene features your child's guide, Hypie the Hummingbird, who asks thoughtful questions, which you can read along with your child to prompt your discussions. You will soon discover that these scenarios can be incorporated into your bedtime routine, or they can be useful for the child to read during time-outs. The best use of these cartoon scenes is when the child is sitting with you and talking about what is happening in each scene. Try to make a habit of setting a little time aside daily to sit and discuss the cartoons with your child. Review the scenarios and practice problem-solving skills. Your child may enjoy coloring the cartoon characters in *The Buzz & Pixie Activity Coloring Book* or may wish to make his or her own drawings.

In addition to the cartoon scenes, we have provided cut-out finger puppets of Buzz, Pixie, and Hypie the Hummingbird for your child to use in imaginative play. Your child can act out each of the situations depicted in the cartoons. These finger puppets can be found in Appendix D.

You will find this chapter to be a useful reference for dealing with your child's behavior. You will also find that talking about Buzz's and Pixie's behavior and their misadventures will be non-threatening, entertaining, and therapeutic for your child.

Situations that Occur at Home

1. Bedtime
2. Misbehaving in front of company
3. Bad table manners
4. Climbing on furniture
5. Breaking toys
6. Getting into things
7. Lying
8. Teasing and fighting with siblings
9. Carelessness in the bathtub
10. Intruding on others
11. Mistreating pets
12. Rough play
13. Interrupting others

Situations at Home (1) Bedtime (Not Going to Sleep)

HYPIE THE HUMMINGBIRD ASKS :

What is happening here? What time is it? Should Buzz be jumping on his bed? Why not? What should Buzz be doing instead? How do his parents feel? What would you do?

Dr. Reimers Explains: Tuck-in Troubles

Buzz is too wound up and is not able to settle down at bedtime. He is very irritable and unwilling to go to sleep. His parents are exhausted and feel frustrated; they've told him three times to go to bed. Instead, Buzz continues to bounce on and off his bed, scattering his toys all over his room.

Winding up at bedtime, rather than winding down, is a common experience with ADHD children. For most children, getting a second wind at night is a natural process, however, with the ADHD child, it is a much more intense experience. It often takes more time for a child with ADHD to go to sleep than a non-ADHD child. Several factors may contribute to an ADHD child's agitation at bedtime. Some medications (prescribed or over-the-counter) can over-stimulate the child before bedtime. Inconsistency in the nightly bedtime schedule could exacerbate the fatigue level, which affects his irritability. Overstimulation prior to bedtime, such as the child's rough play, action movies, emotional conflicts, and others can excite the child. Hunger and certain food may also contribute to sleeplessness.

The goal at bedtime is not necessarily getting the child to sleep immediately, but helping the child relax enough to lay quietly without disturbing others.

HYPIE THE HUMMINGBIRD ASKS :

What is Buzz doing now? How do his
parents feel now? Why? What can you do
to get ready for bed each night?
(Read stories, listen to quiet music, etc.)

Dr. Reimers' Remedies: Tuck-in Troubles

1. Conserve your energy throughout the day so you are relaxed enough to deal with any bedtime agitation. If you are relaxed then your child will be less stimulated by your response.

2. To help conserve your energy throughout the day, use the "tag-team" parenting method. One parent should be responsible for the supervision of the child at specific times, allowing the other parent some time off.

3. Give your child quiet time before coming to bed. Turn off the television prior to going to the bedroom. Provide your child with calming activities (e.g., listening to music, sitting on the bed while reading a story). Sitting with the child in a rocking chair is ideal. The movement back and forth is usually very relaxing for the child.

4. While reading a story, let your child hold something in his hand, allowing him to release excess energy, such as a squeeze ball, silly putty, toy car, stuffed animal, or doll. Try to integrate the object that your child is holding into the story.

5. Specify, in advance, at what time the lights will be turned off. You should also tell your child that he is expected to go to sleep at that time. Allow him or her to continue holding the object in the dark as long as no other rules are broken.

6. Do not let your child take a nap before bed time.

7. Tell your child that his imaginary friend is sleepy and wants to go to bed, too.

Situations at Home (2) Misbehaving in Front of Company

HYPIE THE HUMMINGBIRD ASKS :

What is happening here? What is Buzz doing?
Do the guests like what Buzz is doing? Why not?
How does his mother feel? What do you think
Buzz should do?

Oh No!

Dr. Reimers Explains: The Sideshow Showoff

Buzz has been looking forward to the arrival of guests at his home all day. When the guests arrive, Buzz cannot contain his excitement. He climbs up on top of the couch, behind the guest's heads, and he bumps their heads and shoulders as he scampers along behind them. After jumping off the couch, he repeats the circuit, running around to the other side of the couch and climbing up behind the heads of the guests again. Buzz's mother yells after him for the seventh time, and the guests start to comment angrily, but all this attention only excites him more.

What is Buzz thinking? Is he really trying to embarrass his parentsß in front of their friends? Buzz, like other young children often doesn't understand the reasons for his misbehavior.

The ADHD child's actions are not always consciously motivated, but rather impulsively driven. Whether or not they want more attention or are feeling insecure, transitioning to a new situation overwhelms and overexcites the youngster.

HYPIE THE HUMMINGBIRD ASKS :

What is Buzz doing now? How do his guests feel now? Is his mother happy? Why? Why do you think it is important to behave nicely when guests visit?

Dr. Reimers' Remedies: The Sideshow Showoff

1. Immediately establish the rules of the house: no running, no jumping, use only quiet voices, etc. These rules should be consistent and followed by everyone in the home. Discuss these rules often.

2. Supervise your child closely to prevent him from getting overly excited, making it difficult to settle down. Have the child sit on your lap frequently. Give the child something to play with.

3. Remove your child from the situation whenever he becomes overly excited.

4. Write a simple contract with the child. For example, "Buzz will follow the house rules today. When I do this, I can invite a friend over to play with me tomorrow."

5. Make a checklist of activities that the child is permitted to do, such as looking at books, playing with blocks, etc.

6. Agree upon a recognizable signal that you can give to your child when he is not settling down (e.g., a secret word, hand signal, etc.).

7. Tell your child that his imaginary friend is waiting for him to go to his room and play with him.

8. Enlist your child to help serve the guests.

Situations at Home (3) Bad Table Manners

I DON'T WANT IT!

Uh-Oh!

HYPIE THE HUMMINGBIRD ASKS :

What is happening here? Why is Pixie throwing food? How do her parents feel? How should Pixie behave at the dinner table?

Dr. Reimers Explains: Losing it Over Linguini

Pixie sits at the dinner table while her mom serves the food. Pixie doesn't want to have spaghetti, and starts to whine. Pixie's whining quickly turns into a temper tantrum at the dinner table. What would normally be a pleasant evening is turning into a disaster. Before her dad can say anything, Pixie throws him a spaghetti-filled bowl and knocks over glasses and dishes.

Sometimes parents of children with ADHD can feel very frustrated and helpless at dinnertime. ADHD children's table manners can quickly take a change for the worse similar to a tornado dropping suddenly from the sky and destroying things before you have time to take cover. When the child acts up at the dinner table, often the child wins and the parents lose.

ADHD children often engage in power struggles with their parents. They want to control situations. Negative feedback may anger the child and can worsen behavior, particularly if parents overreact.

HYPIE THE HUMMINGBIRD ASKS :

What is Pixie doing now? How do her parents feel now? Why? What can you do to behave nicely at the dinner table?

Dr. Reimers' Remedies: Losing it Over Linguini

1. Teach proper behavior for home and outdoors in the convenience of your home. For example, whispering in a movie theater, talking quietly at dinner, not screaming when there are disagreements, and not playing with food.

2. Give your child reinforcement for demonstrating appropriate manners at home and in social situations (e.g.,"Your manners were great at dinner. I liked the way you chew your food with your mouth closed.").

3. Use a pretend friend to demonstrate appropriate table manners (e.g., "Look at how Terrance Teddy Bear uses his knife and fork to eat. That's very good Terry.").

4. Reward other family members for appropriate table manners. Parents should serve as an appropriate role model, i.e., do not argue at the table.

5. If your child continues to act up, remove him until he chooses to behave.

6. Always apply the same behavior rules for similar situations (e.g., do not treat the same behavior, such as burping, as cute one day, but impolite the next).

7. Have everything ready to serve before your child sits down for dinner.

8. Encourage your child to have select toys with them at dinner and in restaurants so they can quietly occupy themselves (e.g., books, matchbox cars, coloring books).

9. If you've both had a bad day, calm the child with a movie, television, or a bath.

Situations at Home (4) Climbing on Furniture

HYPIE THE HUMMINGBIRD ASKS :

What is happening here? Why is Pixie on the table? Should she be standing on the table? Why not? How does her mother feel? What do you think will happen next?

Dr. Reimers Explains: Table-Top Tap Dancing

Pixie loves climbing on furniture. One of her favorite pastimes is to leap onto the top of the couch and then jump off the couch onto a nearby chair. However, today Pixie was in search of new conquests. She saw the dining room table, how high it is, and could not resist climbing on top of it. After reaching the top and being very happy with herself, Pixie jumps and jubilantly dances on the tablecloth.

Pixie's tap-dance routine comes to an abrupt end when her mother sees her and shouts, "Pixie! What are you doing up there?" Caught in the act and caught off-balance, Pixie slips on the tablecloth and tumbles off the table.

While most children look before they leap, ADHD kids have difficulty restraining their curiosity. Normal children will sometimes climb on furniture, but ADHD children are driven to climb furniture, bookcases, and cabinets, almost on a daily basis. As a result, parents feel stressed because they feel compelled to watch their children constantly.

HYPIE THE HUMMINGBIRD ASKS :

What is Pixie doing now? How does her mother feel now? Why? What other things should you not climb on? Why? Why is it important to not climb on furniture?

Dr. Reimers' Remedies: Table-Top Tap Dancing

1. Write down the rules for behaving around the house and post them in a conspicuous place (e.g., no walking on any furniture - beds, chairs, or tables).

2. Show positive reinforcement by rewarding other visiting children who follow the rules.

3. Make certain the child is aware of the consequences for his behavior (e.g., "If you jump on the bed, you'll likely wind up sleeping in a broken bed.").

4. Reward the when he listens to you and changes his behavior (e.g., "When you stop climbing on the back of the couch, you can see the Barney® video.").

5. To ensure he has heard you, have your child paraphrase what you said.

6. Don't yell instructions to your child from another room.

7. Be consistent in applying the rules so your child always knows what is expected.

8. The more time you spend supervising your child in all situations, the more responsive he will be to following the rules.

9. Don't criticize, berate or embarrass your child. Just let him know certain behaviors aren't acceptable and move on.

10. When your child is hyper and all else fails, take a break for both of you by going to the playground.

Situations at Home (5) Breaking Toys

Dr. Reimers Explains: The Monster Mash

Buzz is playing with his toy dinosaurs and trucks. He begins to attack the trucks with his dinosaurs. He starts bashing the dinosaurs into the trucks, but soon gets carried away and pretends that he is the dinosaur, smashing the trucks with his feet. Buzz ends up breaking the wheels off and flattening the trucks.

Breaking toys is a common occurrence for an ADHD child. Is it because they are curious, and like to test the physical limits of their toys? Is it because they are impulsive? Is it because they like to see if they can put them back together? Could it be because they are frustrated or angry? Or, is it because they need to get attention from parents because they feel insecure? It is possible that it could be all of these reasons or something entirely different.

ADHD children are often too overexcited, don't know their own strength, and end up breaking their toys. Some children derive a thrill from releasing their energy and venting their feelings, which often results in destructive behavior.

HYPIE THE HUMMINGBIRD ASKS:

What is Buzz doing now? Do you think he is playing with his toys nicely? What is your favorite toy? How should you play with it? Why is it important to care for your toys?

Dr. Reimers' Remedies: The Monster Mash

1. Establish rules for taking care of belongings or toys.

2. If there are any other children or adolescents in the home, reward them for taking good care of their toys and other belongings.

3. Limit your child's use of belongings until he can take care of them properly.

4. Place the broken toys in a pretend "toy hospital." Explain to the child that he will be charged for the toy's hospital stay by giving you tokens, money, or other toys as payment.

5. Give the child old toys that can be taken apart or broken.

6. Provide your child with a list of his belongings and proper ways to care for them.

7. Act as a model for taking care of belongings by doing so yourself (e.g., show how you take care of your car).

8. Have your child place a star or check mark beside each belonging on the list for which he takes proper care and allow your child to exchange the stars or check marks for rewards.

9. Make it clear that the child must replace broken toys. Have the child pay for new toys. Do not buy toys for your child if he does not care for them.

Situations at Home (6) Getting Into Things

Dr. Reimers Explains: The Spot Remover

Pixie is always getting into things. Pixie's parents usually lock all the closets in the house, This time, Pixie's mother forgot to lock one closet because she had taken some carpet cleaner out to remove a spot. After watching her mother remove the spot from the carpet, Pixie gets an idea.

When her mother isn't around, Pixie takes the rug cleaner from the unlocked closet and looks for her puppy. Finding the puppy, Pixie uses the rug cleaner on her puppy's spots. Pixie also adds some laundry bleach, shampoo, laundry detergent, and dishwashing powder to get rid of her puppy's spots.

Pixie's mother runs to the kitchen when she hears the puppy yelping. She finds Pixie sitting on the floor, holding down her puppy, in a frothy mess. And sure enough, Pixie managed to remove a spot or two—along with patches of the puppy's fur!

Many children with ADHD are incredibly bright and inquisitive. It is not uncommon for these kids to explore their environment and experiment with new activities. However, ADHD children are so impulsive that they do not consider the possible consequences of their actions before they try something new.

Dr. Reimers' Remedies: The Spot Remover

1. Establish clear, firm rules about playing in closets or using things without permission.

2. Make sure that the child understands the relationship between the behavior and the consequences, i.e., using bleach on the puppy could hurt him.

3. Along with the rules, provide incentives (e.g., "If you stay out of the closet, you may have a special treat.").

4. Have the child repeat the rules back to you to ensure comprehension.

5. Supervise your child as much as necessary.

6. Make sure that potentially dangerous items are locked away in high cabinets.

7. Enlist the aid of the child's imaginary friend to reinforce safety rules around the house.

8. Have the child draw pictures of the rules to reinforce his understanding (e.g., a picture of an open closet with a big X drawn over it.).

9. Teach the child to self-monitor behavior by asking herself questions. "Should I be getting into this?" "Is this okay to do?" "Is this safe to do?" "What would Mommy and Daddy think?"

10. Together with the child, draw "Danger" or "Poison" labels and have the child put them on dangerous items, as you explain the hazards of playing with the items.

Situations at Home (7) Lying

Dr. Reimers Explains: The Girl Who Cried Wolf

Pixie always wanted to be the center of attention and lying had worked well. Pixie would hit her brother and then would lie and say that he fell. Pixie would also pretend she was ill to try to avoid going to school. One day, Pixie's father injured himself while working on the car engine. Pixie was asked to get help. Pixie told her mother, but this time her mother did not believe her. After finding out what really happened, her mother felt guilty and angry.

Children with ADHD are more emotionally reactive. They demand to be noticed, insist on being the center of attention, and want to belong to the group. They often have poor social skills. They compensate for this by lying to gain peer acceptance. When their efforts to gain attention fail, they often act out to attract negative attention, which is better than none at all.

Lying behavior often takes the form of fake illnesses, lying to get out of trouble, or lying to become the hero. Regardless of the child's motives for lying, parental overreaction will only damage the child's self-esteem and provide the wrong kind of attention. Reacting emotionally also overstimulates the child's brain, making it more difficult for the child to respond appropriately.

Dr. Reimers' Remedies: The Girl Who Cried Wolf

1. Establish a rule for telling the truth. Review it often as situations occur.

2. It is essential to have open and honest communication. Your child shouldn't have any fear or reservations about talking to you.

3. Encourage and reward truthful communication by always (e.g.,"Thank you for telling the truth."). Use other family members as models for telling the truth.

4. Consider children's communication skills when deciding if they have been honest They may omit key facts or just forget.

5. Do not argue about lying with your child. Reframe your position to a more positive perspective.

6. Do not overreact if your child lies. Talk about it calmly and determine why the child lied.

7. Establish realistic chores and responsibilities so your child will not feel pressured to lie.

8. Encourage your children to acknowledge mistakes early, rather than postpone telling you until the problem has escalated.

9. Make sure the punishment for lying fits the crime. Overly severe reprisals could discourage telling the truth.

Situations at Home (8) Teasing/Fighting with Siblings

Dr. Reimers Explains: Sibling Smash

Buzz loves to tease and torment his sister. They are playing in the playroom when Buzz suddenly pounces on her, knocking her down. She cries, and Buzz gets a scolding from his mother. Buzz then gets a ball and throws it at his sister in the hallway. It is a direct hit. Buzz's sister begins to cry and his mother yells at him again and slaps his hand. Later, Buzz runs outside and plays baseball with a plastic bat. After just a few minutes, Buzz takes the bat and smashes his sister with it. Buzz's mother is angry because she cannot get anything done. She feels exhausted from breaking up fights all day long. She also feels guilty about slapping Buzz.

While most children have conflicts with siblings, children with ADHD constantly fight with their brothers and sisters. The fighting is driven by impulsivity, demand for attention, the need for control, misreading social cues, overreacting, impatience, or a low threshold for frustration. Sometimes, the fights may actually be instigated by a sibling, who may be aware of the ADHD child's weaknesses.

Dr. Reimers' Remedies: Sibling Smash

1. Set clear rules (e.g., share toys, do not fight) and review them frequently with the children. Reward them for following the rules.

2. Reward the child for treating his sibling kindly. You could use verbal praise, hugs, kisses, watch a video, or go to a movie with the parent.

3. Rehearse with your children how to behave nicely, share, and use words instead of fists.

4. Teach the child other ways to deal with anger and frustration (e.g., leave the room, talk with a parent, do another activity).

5. Keep the child away from siblings until he/she can treat them respectfully.

6. Show respect for your children. If you don't, they will mistreat others.

7. Make a simple contract with your child: "I, Buzz, will not call my sister names."

8. Do not emphasize competition between siblings.

9. Try to spend more individual time with each child.

10. Use the child's imaginary friend to communicate rules and consequences.

11. Have the child engage in other activities without the sibling.

Situations at Home (9) Bathtub Carelessness

HYPIE THE HUMMINGBIRD ASKS :

What is happening? Why is Pixie splashing and slipping in the tub? How do you think Pixie's mom will feel when she sees the mess in the bathroom? What is the safe way to take a bath?

Dr. Reimers Explains: Tidal Wave in the Tub

Pixie is enjoying her time in the bathtub. She quickly discovers that she can make waves, and rock the boat and other bathtub toys. She starts swirling the water slowly, gradually gaining speed, sending her boat and toys into a whirlpool.

As she picks up speed, the waves get larger and larger. Pixie squeals with delight as the water sloshes up against the wall and spills onto the bathroom floor. In her excitement, Pixie starts to lose control as she stands up and uses her legs to stir the water even faster. Pixie slips and falls down into the tub. A tidal wave of water soars up and over the edge and floods the bathroom floor.

Children with ADHD are driven by intense curiosity. They always want to test the limits of things. Usually, their curiosity and impulsivity eclipse any thoughts about personal safety. Their reaction escalates in tempo with the level of excitement gained from the current activity. For example, Pixie's inability to restrain her wavemaking is due to the increasing excitement she derived from making larger and larger waves. ADHD children live in the moment. They do not consider the consequences of their actions.

HYPIE THE HUMMINGBIRD ASKS :

What is Pixie doing now? Is Pixie having fun in the tub? Why is it important to play safely in the tub? Why is it important to keep the water inside the tub?

Dr. Reimers' Remedies: Tidal Wave in the Tub

1. Set clear rules about bathroom behavior. Explain the dangers and messes that could result from disobeying the rules.

2. Stay with your child to prevent him/her from getting too excited in the tub.

3. Develop a song to keep the child's attention on bathing versus mindless splashing. For example, as the child scrubs her feet, she can progressively sing,, "The toe bone's connected to the foot bone...The foot bone's connected to the leg bone..."

4. Using pretend play, have the child's bath toys interact with each other.

5. As a self-monitoring technique, have the child's imaginary friend indicate when the child is getting too excited.

6. Avoid having more than one child in the tub at a time.

7. Parents can give a special signal when the child is becoming too excited in the tub.

8. Give the child plastic blocks to build an underwater castle.

9. Use shaving cream to make floating "icebergs" and have children maneuver their boats carefully around them. Or, lather the child's face and give him/her a wooden popsicle stick ("shaver") and a child's mirror to shave in the tub.

Situations at Home (10) Intruding on Others

HYPIE THE HUMMINGBIRD ASKS :

What is Buzz doing? How does the guest feel about Buzz coming into the bathroom? What should you do if someone else is using the bathroom?

Dr. Reimers Explains: The Unwelcome Visitor

A friend of the family visiting Buzz's home, is using the restroom. Buzz can't contain his curiosity about what the guest is doing in the bathroom. He decides to investigate. While sitting on the toilet, the guest is shocked when Buzz opens the door, strolls into the bathroom, and asks the guest, "Hi, what are you doing?"

Children with ADHD often lack social graces. They have the aptitude to understand social rules, but because they have short attention spans, they often do not focus on learning the rules.

Impulsivity or poor inhibition of behavior often causes the child to break social rules. As in this example, Buzz was driven by an urgent desire to find out what was going on behind closed doors. His desire overrode any inhibition of his behavior.

Dr. Reimers' Remedies: The Unwelcome Visitor

1. Establish rules for respecting other people's privacy (e.g., knock before you enter, excuse yourself when you barge in on someone). These rules should be reviewed often and followed by everyone.

2. Explain why it is not acceptable to intrude on others (e.g., it embarrasses others, hurts others' feelings, it is disrespectful).

3. Reward your child for not intruding on others.

4. Rehearse appropriate behavior with the child by role playing. (For example, you could go into the bathroom, and close the door. Have the child practice knocking on the door and asking if it is okay to enter. Tell the child that you are using the bathroom, and tell the child to walk away from the door.)

5. Respect your child's privacy. Do not barge into the bathroom when your child is there; ask for permission to enter the child's bedroom.

6. Use the child's imaginary friend to reinforce/remind the child of the rules. For example, if the child has entered the bathroom, you could say, "Laurie, what would Molly do if she came in just now?"

7. Use the child's imaginary friend to redirect the child away from the door to another activity. For example, if the child is barging into your home office while you are working on the computer, you could say, "Laurie, Molly told me that she wants to play with you at the doll house and have a tea party. So get out the dishes, okay?"

Situations at Home (11) Mistreating Pets

Dr. Reimers Explains: A Pet's Worst Friend

Buzz has a pet hamster that he loves dearly. Most of the time, Buzz's parents do not let him handle the hamster. But one day, while his parents were watching TV, Buzz was bored and went to his room to find something to do.

Buzz found a paper cup and string, made two holes in the cup, and tied the string to it to make a long handle. Buzz put his pet hamster in the cup and started twirling the hapless pet around and around. After a minute of this, Buzz released his dizzy hamster onto his bed and laughed as the poor critter staggered around in a daze. Buzz got a plastic bowl and was going to see if his hamster could ride in it like a boat in the toilet. But his parents caught him, just in time.

Some children with ADHD regard their living pets as indestructible toys. The root of the problem is that the child does not consider the consequences or end result of his actions. Empathy requires one to see things from another's perspective. Young children, especially those with ADHD, often do not consider this. In this case, the child is not able to understand that the pet has feelings and that it feels distressed by the child's mistreatment.

Dr. Reimers' Remedies: A Pet's Worst Friend

1. Make rules for taking proper care of your pets (e.g., give them adequate food and water, be gentle, do not tease). Make sure everyone in the house follows the same rules.

2. Practice with the child how to feed and care for the pet. Practice several times with the child before allowing him to take care of the pet.

3. Have a heart-to-heart talk with your child about the fact that the pet has feelings, and does not like to be hurt or mistreated. Help the child understand by asking empathetic questions such as, "How would you feel if someone pulled your hair, or stepped on your foot?"

4. Reward your child for treating the pet kindly.

5. Point out to the child when the pet expresses affection, saying that this is how the pet says "thank you."

6. Help the child understand the relationship between actions and consequences (e.g., teasing the cat will make him angry, and he'll scratch your face.).

7. Remind your child when you see him starting to play too roughly with the pet.

8. Allow your child to show his pet to friends, which may help the child bond closer with the pet.

Situations at Home (12) Rough Play

Dr. Reimers Explains: Demolition Derby

While playing with a friend, Buzz has discovered a new way to use his toy cars—bumps and crashes. Buzz enlists his friend to begin with a couple of cars crashing.

Then Buzz gets more excited, and starts throwing the cars across the room at Johnny. Johnny gets into the act, too, and soon the air is filled with tiny toy cars criss-crossing between the two boys. But their fun screeches to a halt when Buzz throws a car and scores a direct hit on Johnny's eye. Oblivious to Johnny's eye injury, Buzz laughingly continues throwing more cars at him.

ADHD boys, in particular, are notorious for rough play. Typically, play activities escalate out of control and often result in injury. The kids are not intentionally malicious, but they don't read important social cues. They get carried away with excitement even after their playmates get hurt. They may not show the empathy or concern for the other child that would make their aggressive behavior a little more acceptable.

Dr. Reimers' Remedies: Demolition Derby

1. Set rules for playing gently with toys and with others. For example, when playing with toy cars, no cars should hit other's arms, heads, etc.

2. Play with your child and show him or her how to play appropriately with the toys.

3. Reward or praise the child for playing nicely with toys: "You're taking such good care of your cars. We can go buy some more to add to your collection."

4. Remind him of the rules. Check on your child and don't allow vigorous play to escalate out of control.

5. Make a simple contract with the child which emphasizes rewards and consequences. Fore example, "I, Buzz, will play nicely with my toy cars. If I break my toy cars, all the other cars will be taken away for a day. If I do not break my cars, I will be able to buy a new toy car."

6. Try to invite friends over who play gently with toys so your child will learn from a positive role model.

7. Teach empathy. Discuss with your child how a playmate would feel if your child played too rough.

8. Tell the child that lost or destroyed toys must be paid for by the child out of his/her own piggy bank, or that the child must do chores to compensate for it.

Situations at Home (13) Interrupting Others

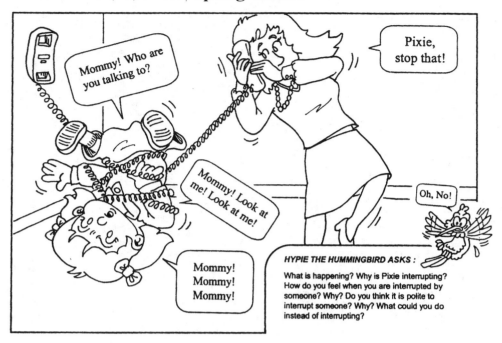

HYPIE THE HUMMINGBIRD ASKS :

What is happening? Why is Pixie interrupting? How do you feel when you are interrupted by someone? Why? Do you think it is polite to interrupt someone? Why? What could you do instead of interrupting?

Dr. Reimers Explains: Interruptions, Interruptions

Pixie's mother is on the telephone. Pixie plays with the telephone cord, wrapping it around her body. She falls down, tugs the cord, and almost pulls the phone from her mother's hand.

Other times, Pixie sings a nursery song loudly or pesters her mom by saying, "Mom...Mom!" over and over. Whenever guests come to visit, Pixie is always there. She jumps into the conversation or asks pesky questions until her mother has to tell Pixie to stop interrupting.

It's quite normal for young children to interrupt others, but children with ADHD seem to do an inordinate amount of interrupting. Sometimes, it seems that they just want to be noticed, other times they want to be included in the action, and much of the time it is because they simply do not know how to behave in certain social situations.

Many parents do not realize that when they pay attention to a child who interrupts, they are rewarding that behavior. Conversely, they pay little attention when the child isn't interrupting or is playing independently.

Dr. Reimers' Remedies: Interruptions, Interruptions

1. Establish rules about interrupting when you are on the phone, cooking meals, watching TV, or any other activities.

2. Help the child understand how you and others feel when the child interrupts.

3. Teach the child how to wait for her turn. Do reverse role playing, with you as the interrupting child and your child as the "adult." Then ask the child what the correct behavior should have been. Next, you can do realistic rehearsals. Tell the child that you are going to call someone on the phone, and you do not want to be interrupted. Then call a friend on the phone to see if the child can resist interrupting you.

4. If you know ahead of time that you are going to be doing something, such as talking on the phone, working on the computer, or fixing a meal, then prepare a special task for the child to keep him/her busy. Some examples include setting up activity spots for the child, putting on a video, or giving the child a new book to read.

5. Reward or praise your child for not interrupting.

6. Provide your child with frequent opportunities to be included in conversations.

7. Teach the child that the only proper time to interrupt is during an emergency.

8. Do not keep your child waiting for more than a minute to talk with you.

Situations That Occur at School

1. Pushing in line
2. Fighting at school
3. Lack of eye contact
4. Grabbing things from others
5. Not staying with classroom tasks
6. Misbehaving in the circle
7. Short attention span
8. Obeying the rules of play
9. Playground misbehavior
10. Misinterpreting friendly teasing
11. Talkativeness
12. Making noises
13. Hyperactivity

Situations at School (1) Pushing in Line

Dr. Reimers Explains: Little Dominoes

Buzz and his classmates line up to go outside to play. Buzz is bored waiting in line, and to entertain himself, he starts pushing the child in front of him. After one particularly strong push, Buzz makes the child fall down, knocking over the rest of the children in the line like a set of dominoes.

Pushing, tugging, and touching are common behaviors in which ADHD children engage, especially when they have to wait. It is important to understand that waiting behavior causes frustration because of the restraint necessary to stay still. When told to wait, the child may feel much like a spinning top unable to stop. All of the energy pent up in the child continues to be expressed through movement.

Dr. Reimers' Remedies: Little Dominoes

1. Anticipation is the key with ADHD children, especially during times of transition. Inform your student what will be expected of him or her. Discuss such issues as:
    a. The rules before transitioning to a new activity.
    b. Specific rewards for good behavior.
    c. Punishments for misbehaving.
    Above all, the teacher must follow through on these expectations.

2. Establish rules of behavior for waiting in line. Make them simple!

3. Before having the child wait in line, review the rules for appropriate behavior.

4. Give your child a task to do while waiting in line, such as handing out water cups to the other children.

5. Give the child a special object to play with while standing in line, such as a stop watch. The object should only be used when standing in line so that it effectively functions as a transitional object.

6. Write a simple contract with the child. For example, "I, Jack, will not touch or push others in line or I will have to wait in the time-out area."

7. Closely supervise the child and give verbal reinforcers for on-target behavior.

Situations at School (2) Fighting at School

Dr. Reimers Explains: Feisty Fists

Jack and Buzz are constructing a castle from building blocks. Jack wants to use a toy dumptruck to transport some building blocks to the construction site, but Buzz is using the dumptruck. Jack asks Buzz several times if he can borrow the truck, but Buzz is too distracted with the truck to hear Jack. Jack feels that it is now his turn to use the truck, and he takes it from Buzz. Enraged, Buzz immediately retaliates by punching Jack, grabbing the truck away, and biting Jack on his arm.

Children with ADHD often respond aggressively because they misread social cues and interpret events as black and white. The shades of gray (such as negotiating for sharing) are difficult to discern. Their fighting is often an impulsive reaction, and seems as if it explodes out of nowhere. The emotional outburst may go beyond mere retaliation and on to primal, unbridled revenge. As in this example, Buzz acted impulsively without considering why Jack took the truck. Buzz misinterpreted the situation. Jack's intent was to increase the size of the castle they were both working on.

Dr. Reimers' Remedies: Feisty Fists

1. Establish rules for getting along with others (e.g., choose your words, play cooperatively). Talk about the rules often in class.

2. Reward the child for not fighting.

3. Show the child how to avoid fighting with others (e.g., play cooperatively, share, talk in an acceptable manner, do not threaten others).

4. Do not allow the child to play with children with whom he fights.

5. Do not emphasize competitive activities because they may cause the child to fight. Prosocial games should be encouraged.

6. Talk with the child about appropriate ways to deal with anger and frustration (e.g., compromise, walk away from the situation, talk with an adult about the problem).

7. Make certain that the child understands the relationship between his behavior and the consequences that follow (i.e., losing friends, having to stay in during recess, being suspended from school).

8. Arrange for the child to be involved in many activities with other children so the skills necessary for appropriate interaction may be learned and practiced.

Situations at School (3) Lack of Eye Contact

> Pixie, please pay attention when I'm talking to you!

> Uh-Oh!

HYPIE THE HUMMINGBIRD ASKS :

What is happening here? Why is Pixie not looking at her teacher? Why is it important to look at someone when she talks to you? How do you think Pixie's teacher feels?

Dr. Reimers Explains: Wandering Eyes

Here we see the teacher trying to talk to Pixie, but she is easily distracted. Instead of looking into at the teacher, Pixie's eyes wander and are drawn toward a doll. Pixie may actually be listening to the teacher's words, but her body language indicates otherwise. The teacher is frustrated with Pixie for not paying attention.

Listening requires good attention. Requiring an ADHD child to listen attentively often results in frustration. For the easily distracted child, focusing one's attention is much like shooting arrows aimlessly at a number of different targets. Because of their unfocused, aimless, and short attention spans, these children are often labeled as spacey. Many of them cannot tell the difference between essential and nonessential information. They get bored quickly and distracted by anything that might be more stimulating or interesting. Thus, the greater challenge for children with ADHD is when they are faced with unexciting, unwanted tasks and activities, such as chores or listening to lectures.

Dr. Reimers' Remedies: Wandering Eyes

1. If the child is having difficulty maintaining eye contact, you can place a small object (such as a ball) on the child's nose, then move it toward your nose to encourage eye contact. This may seem silly to an adult, but for young kids, this is a great method for eliciting desired behavior.

2. Offer praise when the child listens attentively.

3. Requiring eye contact can sometimes turn into a power struggle. Instead, ask the child to repeat what you've said to check comprehension.

4. Find a quiet part of the classroom (or hallway), sit down at the child's level, and talk.

5. Prior to talking with the child, remove any objects nearby that could distract him or her.

6. When talking with the child, keep your conversation brief.

7. When giving directions to the class, move closer to children with ADHD so they can see you without difficulty.

8. Use different ways (auditory, visual, tactile, etc.) to captivate the child's attention while you are talking.

Situations at School (4) Grabbing Things from Others

Dr. Reimers Explains: The Little Swiper

Pixie sees a boy in her class reading one of her favorite books. She feels that it is her book, and no one else has a right to touch it. She wants the book, so she walks over and swipes it away from the boy without asking for it. The boy tries to take it back, and a tug-of-war starts. The teacher has to intervene before the two kids destroy the book.

Due to their heightened emotional state and level of arousal, children with ADHD are sometimes overpossessive regarding certain items they like. Most have a poor repertoire of social skills for negotiating disputes, so they tend to grab things away from others impulsively. This aggressive behavior may result in fights, and the child will usually blame another child for starting it. The ADHD child seldom sees the relationship between cause and effect.

Dr. Reimers' Remedies: The Little Swiper

1. Set the rules for sharing in the classroom, such as playing nicely, asking permission to borrow things, etc.

2. Role play some situations to demonstrate proper sharing. Help the child practice how to react properly when a classmate says "no."

3. Point out other exemplary children in the class who exhibit good sharing behavior.

4. Explain the consequences of grabbing things from others (e.g., no one will want to play with the child, feelings will be hurt).

5. If you see the child forcefully take items away from others, make sure the child returns them immediately.

6. Teach the child ways of handling anger (e.g., walking away from the situation, talking it over with the teacher, doing a different activity).

7. Keep the child away from other children with whom he/she has trouble sharing.

8. When the child is successful at sharing, reward the child with a favorite toy that he or she previously had difficulty sharing.

Situations at School (5) Not Staying with Class Tasks

HYPIE THE HUMMINGBIRD ASKS :

What is Buzz doing? Why? Do you think Buzz is bored? What should you do when your teacher gives you something to do? How do you think the teacher feels when Buzz doesn't do his schoolwork?

Dr. Reimers Explains: The Wandering Cowboy

Here we find Buzz wandering aimlessly around the classroom, participating in any given activity for only a few minutes. In a 10 minute period, Buzz visited the block area, the painting easel, the housekeeping area, the reading corner, and the computer station. He interacted only superficially with the other children at each site, and always leaves unfinished activities in his wake. During group time, Buzz becomes bored quickly and leaves the circle several times to visit other parts of the classroom. A teacher's aid feels compelled to follow Buzz around the room to ensure that he does not disturb the circle time.

Children with ADHD often move about the classroom and have extreme difficulty staying seated, especially during group activity. The scene is often reminiscent of a wandering cowboy drifting aimlessly, lost among the cattle. Since these children have decreased self-control, asking them to sit still and pay attention may not have much impact.

HYPIE THE HUMMINGBIRD ASKS :

What is Buzz doing now? Is he having fun? Why is it important to finish things that you work on in school? If you feel bored with an activity in class, what should you do?

Dr. Reimers' Remedies: The Wandering Cowboy

1. Try various groupings of activities to determine which ones are motivating. This will help the child attend to the task.

2. Supervise the child. The teacher and child should be able to see each other, making it easier to maintain eye contact.

3. Reinforce the child for staying involved in the activity for a certain length of time and gradually increase the time.

4. Interact frequently with the child to maintain his/her attention to the activity. For example, you may ask the child questions or ask the child's opinion.

5. Give the child additional responsibilities, such as chores or errands to give a feeling of success or accomplishment.

6. Suggest ways to extend the theme of the activity that the child is currently engaged in. For example, if the child is in the dress-up area, pretending to be a cowboy, suggest that he "rustle" the cattle from one place to another in the classroom or build a corral in the block area.

7. Identify a peer who stays in his/her seat to act as a model for the ADHD child.

8. Provide the child with frequent opportunities to participate, take turns, etc., to keep him/her involved in the activity. Stay beside the child during the activity to encourage completion.

Situations at School (6) Misbehaving in the Circle

NYAH, NYAH, CAN'T CATCH ME! HA-HA-HA!

Oh, No!

HYPIE THE HUMMINGBIRD ASKS :

What is Buzz doing? Is Buzz supposed to be disturbing the circle? How does the teacher feel? How do the other children feel? How should you behave when you're sitting in the circle? What do you think will happen to Buzz?

Dr. Reimers Explains: The Circle Circus

The class is sitting in a circle, listening to the teacher read a story. Buzz quickly becomes tired from concentrating on the story and starts rocking back and forth in his chair. He rocks his chair forward until he is in the center of the circle, enjoying the laughter from his classmates. Then he moves his chair next to another child, knocking that child over. The child gets angry and starts chasing Buzz around the circle. The teacher begins chasing the two boys and the children all laugh.

The scene looks like a three-ring circus to the exasperated teacher, who is attempting to regain control. The child with ADHD is often on stage, but not necessarily by choice. The impulsiveness, fidgeting, and short attention span are often a recipe for spontaneous comedic situations that are disruptive to the class. Circle time is often the most difficult time for the teacher to maintain control of ADHD children. It takes a great deal of mental effort to sustain attention or focus on what the teacher is saying. We often take it for granted, since it comes so naturally for us. The task is further compounded when the child is asked to sit or stand in line while paying attention.

HYPIE THE HUMMINGBIRD ASKS :

What is Buzz doing now? How do the
teacher and other children feel? Why?
Why is it important to sit quietly in the
circle?

Dr. Reimers' Remedies: The Circle Circus

1. Remember to redirect your frame of mind by allowing your anger to be turned into humor. Putting things into perspective helps you to deal with situations that feel out of control.

2. You can use this opportunity to redirect the incident into an activity that lets you regain control, such as a game of "duck, duck, goose." If the two children wish to play, they must apologize to each other and demonstrate good sitting behavior outside the circle forthree minutes. Only when they have demonstrated good behavior can they participate in the game.

3. Reinforce the child with tangible rewards for staying seated (class privileges, passing out materials) or intangible rewards (praise, smile, high-five, thumbs up, etc.)

4. Have the child sit on the teacher's lap or next to the teacher.

5. Give the child something small to hold while sitting in the circle.

6. Identify a peer, who is seated, as a model for the ADHD child to imitate. Separate the child from the peer who stimulates the child's bad behavior.

7. Have the child tap his/her imaginary friend on the shoulder and tell it "you'd better stay seated because you need to learn and respect others."

8. Interact frequently with the child to maintain his/her attention (ask questions, ask the child's opinion).

Situations at School (7) Short Attention Span

Dr. Reimers Explains: The Short-Order Cook

Pixie is in the kitchen area of the classroom. Soon three other girls join Pixie, and they pretend to be customers at Pixie's "restaurant." Pixie happily takes their orders, but with her short attention span, she forgets what they ordered by the time she returns to her kitchen. Instead of preparing the "meals," Pixie notices that some dishes are dirty. After that, she arranges the dishes in the cupboard and puts leftover foods in the refrigerator. Meanwhile, Pixie's three "customers" wonder what's taking so long. They grow weary of waiting, and leave to play somewhere else. By this time, Pixie remembers to make three meals, although not the same ones that her customers ordered. She returns to the table with the food, but wonders where her customers have gone.

Unlike a short-order cook, who pays attention to each incoming order, the child with ADHD attends to any activity with a short attention span and forgets simple details. Distractibility often interferes with keeping focused long enough to complete tasks.

Dr. Reimers' Remedies: The Short-Order Cook

1. Add details to the pretend play theme. For example, if the child is playing in the kitchen area, have the child pretend to be a cook for the president, and prepare several meals for all the senators and diplomats. Then you could initiate a discussion about the types of food that are served in different countries.

2. Reinforce the child for paying attention. Use tangible rewards (class privileges, line leading, passing out materials) or intangible rewards (verbal praise, pat on the back, smiles).

3. Reinforce the child for paying attention for a certain length of time. Gradually increase the time as the child achieves success.

4. Provide the child with a predetermined signal or cue when he/she does not pay attention.

5. Have the child repeat directions you've given. Work alongside the child and interact with the child to encourage paying attention. Try various ways of giving instructions to determine which method helps the child pay attention most effectively.

6. Encourage the child to ask questions about anything he/she does not understand before starting an activity. Maintain visibility and eye contact with the child.

7. The teacher can create an imaginary helper for the class, who can convey instructions or lessons. The teacher (through the imaginary helper) can quiz the child to confirm if the child was paying attention.

Situations at School (8) Obeying the Rules of Play

HYPIE THE HUMMINGBIRD ASKS :

What is happening here? Is Buzz following the rules of games? How do the other kids feel about Buzz? Why is it important to follow the rules of games and play nicely with others? Do you think the other kids will let Buzz play with them next time? Why not?

Dr. Reimers Explains: No Rules, No Games, No Friends

Out in the school play yard, the children are playing kickball. Buzz runs into the game and steals the ball. The other children get annoyed and after they take the ball back, they refuse to let Buzz play in their game.

In a game of freeze tag with some other children, Buzz pushes kids to the ground in the midst of his excitement. The other children tell Buzz to "get lost." He then decides to join another group of children who are playing hop-scotch. Instead of throwing the stone onto the squares, he kicks it, and runs off laughing. By the end of the recess, Buzz wonders why he is always alone at playtime.

Following rules, especially social rules, is very difficult because ADHD children can be very impulsive. As a result, they may play too roughly or fail to follow the rules. Thus children with ADHD often get shunned from group activities or common games. ADHD children may not pick up on the cues from their playmates when they behave inappropriately. When they are ostracized, they may lash out in frustration or anger, making things even worse.

Dr. Reimers' Remedies: No Rules, No Games, No Friends

1. Make sure the child understands the rules of games and the social etiquette that goes with them (e.g., taking turns, sharing, no fighting)

2. Explain the consequences of not following the rules of games (e.g., will not be allowed to play the game, other children won't want to play with the child).

3. Praise another child in the class who follows the rules of games and have the ADHD child be his/her partner or coach.

4. Try to avoid competitive games whenever possible, or change the rules of competitive games to de-emphasize winning. Instead, try hide-and-seek or follow the leader games.

5. In any game, emphasize having fun, getting along with others, and doing one's best.

6. Teach the child proper ways to handle frustration during games so the child won't have the urge to cheat or disrupt the game.

7. Choose games that are easy to play and that have simple rules.

8. Supervise the ADHD child during the game to ensure he stays involved. Praise the ADHD child during the game to build self-confidence.

9. When a child masters a certain game at school, encourage the child to play it at home. Have the child teach the rules to other members of the family.

Situations at School (9) Playground Misbehavior

Dr. Reimers Explains: The Playground Prison

Buzz, as always, enjoys the freedom of the playground. He happily runs from place to place, throwing his whole energy into play. Buzz runs and dives onto swings, or he swings really high, lets go, and falls on all fours. Buzz climbs up the slide against the downward flow of the other kids and then slides down head-first. He laughs out loud all the way as he crashes into the other kids at the bottom.

The teacher has warned Buzz several times about playing safely on the playground equipment, and she often has to make Buzz take numerous time-outs. As a result, Buzz feels that the school yard is more of a prison than a playground.

For most children, the playground is a place to be safe and free. For the child with ADHD, however, the playground is anything but safe and free. They often take risks and are more likely to injure themselves due to their impulsivity. Playgrounds can be a place of frustration, confusion, rejection, and shame for the child who is different.

Because play time is usually more exciting, less structured, and less closely supervised by adults, children with ADHD are more likely to misbehave. The playground can become an emotional prison as the child is constantly pulled away to take time-outs.

Dr. Reimers' Remedies: The Playground Prison

1. Establish and review the playground rules with the child. Start with three rules to make them easier to remember. For example,nNo standing on the slide, no climbing on the fence and no pushing.

2. Praise or reward the child for being careful on the playground.

3. When you see the child misbehaving, explain what the child was doing wrong, the consequences, and the proper behavior you would like to see. For example, when you see the child going headfirst down the slide, take the child aside and explain that it is dangerous, that the child could hurt himself or others, and the other children won't want to play with him. Ask the child to try again, demonstrating proper ways to use the slide.

4. Supervise the child closely to prevent any escalation of risky behavior.

5. Impose some structure on the overall flow of the play in the playground; redirect the child to other play activities. For example, if you see the child is running around recklessly between the swings or bumping other children redirect the child to a more structured activity such as making mudpies.

6. Have the child's pretend friend teach him/her how to play safely on the playground equipment. Discuss games that the child's pretend friend can play with the child.

7. Do not let the child play on certain playground equipment unless he or she can first demonstrate how to play safely.

Situations at School (10) Misinterpreting Friendly Teasing

Dr. Reimers Explains: A Touchy Situation

During free-play time in class, one of Buzz's classmates, Joey, is calling everyone "bop heads." Joey happily jumps around the room and sings the children's song, "Little Bunny Foo-Foo," while patting children on their heads.

Joey runs by Buzz and taps him on the head. Buzz is greatly irritated by being patted on the head and reacts angrily for being called a "bop head." Buzz hurls a blood-curdling scream at Joey.

ADHD children react quickly and often do not think through the alternatives to any behavior. Social cues are constantly misinterpreted. The other children interpreted Joey's action as silly and funny. But Buzz, on the other hand, was not able to interpret the context or the intent of Joey's name-calling. In addition, some children with ADHD are oversensitive to tactile stimulation and are greatly irritated when touched, hugged, or bumped.

Dr. Reimers' Remedies: A Touchy Situation

1. Discuss with the child about how to respond appropriately to friendly teasing. Explain that friendly teasing is one way that some people show that they like someone.

2. Role play some joking or teasing scenarios with the child to help him/her recognize friendly teasing and unfriendly teasing.

3. Reward the child for reacting to teasing in an acceptable way.

4. Explain to the child that there are topics which are not acceptable for teasing such as handicaps, poverty, personal appearance, death, and illness.

5. Help the child understand that friendly teasing is a part of having friends.

6. The teacher could give a lesson using puppet shows or role plays to the whole class about teasing.

7. Have the imaginary friend talk about the child's feelings at being teased.

8. Help the child build self-esteem by making positive comments.

9. Do not criticize the child for reacting to friendly teasing.

10. Do not overindulge the child when he/she is teased because it only reinforces the child's sensitivity, and it does not allow the child to deal with teasing independently.

Situations at School (11) Talkativeness

Dr. Reimers Explains: "The Talkaholic"

During circle time, the teacher is reading the story of the Three Little Pigs. Throughout the reading of the story, Pixie interrupts the teacher over and over with a number of pesky questions, "Teacher, what was that house made of again?" "Teacher, why is the big bad wolf blowing their house down?" "How can the wolf blow the houses down?" "Teacher, could you go back and show the picture of the straw house again?" In addition to annoying the teacher during the storytime, Pixie turns to classmates sitting next to her and tries to engage them in conversation.

Excessive talking is a common characteristic of children with ADHD. They are often described as "being driven by a motor...which runs their mouth." Like fidgety limbs, an ADHD child's voice may be an outlet for releasing excess energy. Since this is not under the child's conscious control, teachers should realize that the child has trouble remaining quiet.

Dr. Reimers' Remedies: The Talk-aholic

1. Reward the child for talking at appropriate times in the classroom.

2. Tell the child when there is too much talking.

3. Announce classroom rules in advance (e.g., listen when others are talking, do not interrupt). Repeat the rules and reinforce other children for following the rules.

4. When the child cannot stop talking, remove him or her from the group or activity.

5. Point out when the child talks beyond what is expected, or when the child talks at inappropriate times. Give the child a cue to signal too much talking.

6. Redirect the child's talkativeness by having the child lead a small group activity. Give the child more responsibilities in the classroom (e.g., be the teacher's helper, run errands, allow the child to teach a short lesson).

7. Structure the environment to limit opportunities for interruptions and excessive talking (e.g., keep the child busy, have the child sit next to the teacher). Encourage the child to raise his/her hand to be recognized and to wait before speaking.

8. Interact with the child often to decrease the child's compulsion to interrupt you or other children.

Situations at School (12) Making Noises

Buzz, what are you doing?!

Oh, No!

HYPIE THE HUMMINGBIRD ASKS :

What is Buzz doing? Why is he being noisy? How do his teacher and friends feel? Do you like to be around noisy people? Why not? Why is it important to play without making a lot of noise? What are ways that you can make noise? (with your voice, with your feet, hands, etc.)

Dr. Reimers Explains: The Noise Machine

Buzz is humming, tapping, screeching, and burping as he works on a group project at school. Whenever Buzz talks, he has only two volume settings: "Loud" or "Off." The teacher is frequently reminding Buzz to "use your inside voice." The children are painting pictures but Buzz is noisily using his paintbrush as a drumstick. Of all the children in his class, Buzz's voice is the loudest, and he is often heard down the hall.

Why do ADHD children make strange noises. Impulsivity is part of the reason, ADHD children feel compelled to produce noises or talk loudly. Making noises or yelling can also be a way of letting off steam or excess energy. For some children, making noises simply helps them concentrate better on a task

Dr. Reimers' Remedies: The Noise Machine

1. Set rules about noisemaking in the classroom (e.g., using "inside voices" when indoors). Review the rules each day with the child.

2. Reward the child for following the rules about noisemaking.

3. Show the child other children in the class who are not noisy.

4. Remove the child from the group or classroom until he/she can be quiet.

5. Give the child opportunities to make appropriate noises with his voice, instruments, or objects.

6. Separate the child from any classmate who influences the child to be noisy.

7. Find out what stimuli or events cause the child to become noisy. Structure the classroom environment to reduce or eliminate those stimuli.

8. Intervene early to prevent the child from getting too silly or escalating in noisy behavior. Redirect the child to more quiet activities.

9. Demonstrate to the child how to sit quietly, how to work quietly, or wait quietly in line.

10. Give the child a cue to increase self-awareness about getting too noisy.

Situations at School (13) Hyperactivity

Dr. Reimers Explains: The Jumping Bean

Buzz hops, skips, and jumps. He does anything but walk when moving from one place to another in the classroom. Buzz seems incapable of moving quietly; he is compelled to swing his arms when he walks, fidgets in his chair, and seems off-balance when he moves around the room. As a result, Buzz often bumps into furniture or classmates throughout the day.

ADHD children are the rightful heirs of the Energizer Bunny™ tagline, "just keeps going, and going, and going..." because they never seem to wind down. They cannot inhibit their behavior as well as other children. They are often driven to wiggle, bump, jump, stomp, or hop when moving from place to place.

Dr. Reimers' Remedies: The Jumping Bean

1. Praise the child for walking carefully alone or with a group. Gradually increase the length of time for the child to demonstrate on-target walking behavior.

2. When the child is walking in a line with classmates, stop the line periodically to praise the child and give an opportunity for the child to calm down.

3. Give positive feedback to the child for waiting quietly in lines.

4. Praise the child for walking at the same pace as the other children in the line.

5. Separate the child from classmates who cause the child to escalate out of control. Remove the child from the group or classroom if he/she loses control. Redirect the child to an activity that channels excess energy.

6. Show the child how to move appropriately around the classroom, without bumping anyone or anything. Have the child practice with you. Have the child pair up with another child when moving as a group.

7. Make sure that the child has enough physical outlets for his/her energy throughout the school day.

8. Have the child be first in line, holding your hand, when walking with the class in line.

Other Situations Outside the Home or School

1. Misbehaving in waiting rooms
2. Misbehaving in the car
3. At the grocery store
4. At the movie theater
5. Bowel accidents
6. At a fast food restaurant
7. Losing things
8. At the shopping mall
9. On an airplane
10. Birthday parties
11. Playing with sticks
12. Misusing other's belongings
13. At the swimming pool
14. Misinterpreting social cues
15. Getting lost at the store

Other Situations (1) Misbehaving in Waiting Rooms

HYPIE THE HUMMINGBIRD ASKS :

What are Buzz & Pixie doing in the doctor's waiting room? How does the doctor feel about Buzz and Pixie making a mess in his waiting room? What do you think will happen next? Why? What can you do to behave nicely in waiting rooms?

Dr. Reimers Explains: Waiting Room Riot

Buzz and Pixie are with their mother at the doctor's office. While in the waiting room, Buzz and Pixie begin to play a game of tag, jumping on and off the furniture, as they chase each other. In just a few minutes the room becomes a disaster, with magazines and cushions strewn all over the floor, lamps and plants knocked over, and toys scattered everywhere. As their mother cleans up the mess, she is terribly embarrassed by the frowns she gets from the receptionist and other patients in the room.

ADHD children do not have the ability to wait for long periods of time, since the power to wait is dependent upon the ability to inhibit immediate urges. The inhibition required for waiting takes a great deal of conscious effort. Furthermore, because of the child's distractibility, he or she can easily forget about waiting and get drawn into a more stimulating activity, which often escalates out of control.

HYPIE THE HUMMINGBIRD ASKS :

What are Buzz & Pixie doing now? How does the doctor feel? Why is it important to wait quietly? If you had to wait for a long time, what would you do so that you won't be noisy?

Dr. Reimers' Remedies: Waiting Room Riot

1. Before going to a waiting room establish clear rules about proper behavior and explain what consequences or rewards will follow.

2. Bring along toys, coloring books, puzzles, and other materials to keep the child occupied while waiting.

3. When you arrive, try to sit in the most empty part of the waiting room so the child will not be distracted or overly stimulated while you wait. Use a predetermined signal or cue when the child is having difficulty settling down.

5. If the child becomes too excited, remove him/her from the waiting room for a "time-out" to review the rules and allow time for the child to calm down.

6. Have the child read a story to the imaginary friend. Read your child a story while waiting.

7. Keep a secret "surprise toy" or special snack hidden away in your purse or in a bag. Bring it out to get the child's attention when his behavior is about to escalate out of control.

8. In advance, prepare stapled sheets of blank paper on which the child will draw stories while waiting in the room.

9. Remain calm (in demeanor and voice) when your child is out of control. Do not embarrass the child in front of others.

Other Situations (2) Misbehaving in the Car

Dr. Reimers Explains: The Backseat Nuisance

Buzz is riding in the back seat of the car with his parents. Buzz hates the restricted feeling of the seat belt and quietly takes it off without his parents noticing. He turns around in his seat, facing backward to watch the other cars following behind his. Buzz hears the unmistakable sound of a package of potato chips being ripped open in the front seat by his mother. Buzz, not wanting to miss out on some potato chips, hollers for his mom to share some. Climbing over the front seat, Buzz bumps his mother's hand, sending a burst of potato chips out the window, while his feet kick his father's face, almost causing a car accident.

Parents often feel that ADHD kids are in the driver's seat. For an energetic child, riding in a car can be very confining. ADHD children have an overall developmental delay in self-control, so its hardly surprising that they quickly become backseat nuisances. Their impulsivity causes them to act without considering consequences and dangers, such as undoing one's seatbelt and climbing over seats.

Dr. Reimers' Remedies: The Backseat Nuisance

1. As in all situations, establish clear rules, rewards, and consequences for riding in the car.

2. Give verbal praise to the child (as well as other children riding in the car) for keeping the rules.

3. If another adult is driving, you can sit next to the child to help him/her be successful at following the rules.

4. Provide things to keep your child busy while riding such as coloring books, toys, comic books, or other reading materials.

5. Redirect the child by asking him/her to help you notice signs, other cars, signal lights, etc.

6. If your child loses self-control, pull over, stop the car, and take a time out. Do not try to discipline your child while you are driving.

7. Use a cue or signal to let the child know when he/she is starting to act inappropriately.

8. Appoint your child as the "safety expert" of the car. He reminds everyone to buckle up, make sure that doors are locked, mirrors are adjusted, and check the gas gauge.

9. Tell others (relatives, friends) about the appropriate behavior you expect from your child, so they can encourage your child to behave appropriately when the child rides with them.

Other Situations (3) At the Grocery Store

Dr. Reimers Explains: The Shopping Cart Shocker

Pixie is accompanying her mother to the grocery store. Sitting in the seat of the shopping cart, Pixie looks around and sees a bag of cookies in the front of the shopping cart. Pixie clambers out of the seat and tries to reach for the bag of cookies, precariously tipping the shopping cart as her mother looks on, horrified.

ADHD children are often risk-takers. They are not frightened by things that would normally intimidate other children. Even after a serious fall from the shopping cart, the child will usually tip the cart again. They do not stop and think about safety before doing something. In this example, Pixie is completely focused on the bag of cookies, and she is oblivious to the danger of falling off the cart.

Dr. Reimers' Remedies: The Shopping Cart Shocker

1. Before entering the store, review the rules for behaving in the store.

2. If the child gets out of control in the shopping cart, or runs dangerously through the aisles, remove the child and take a time-out. Review the rules as you wait until the child calms down.

3. Give instructions in a calm, supportive manner instead of using an angry or threatening tone. For example, say "Please sit down!" instead of "You had better sit down or you're going to get it!"

4. Interact with the child while you shop, giving much needed attention. Keep your child busy by asking the child to help you pick items off the shelves or unload the cart at the checkout counter.

5. If the child starts to stand up in the shopping cart, redirect him/her by saying, "We're going to play a game, but you need to sit down safely in order to play."

6. Reward the child for following the rules and demonstrating good behavior by giving treats in the store. There should be enough of the treats so the child can be kept busy eating while you are shopping.

7. Give the child a predetermined signal to let him know when the behavior is escalating.

8. Get your child's "wiggles" out before you take the child shopping. Jumping jacks, trampolines, a trip to the park, or other physical activities help release that extra energy.

Other Situations (4) At The Movie Theater

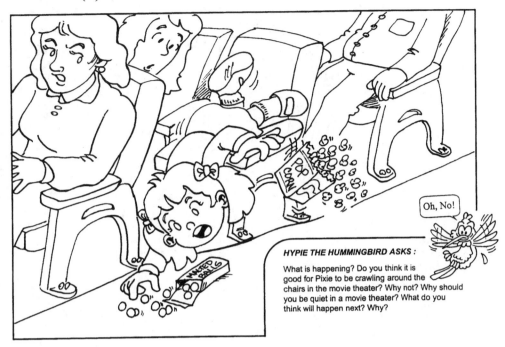

Dr. Reimers Explains: Movie Madness

Pixie and her parents go to the movies. Her parents buy popcorn, drinks, and candy. They all sit down and watch the movie. Within the first 10 minutes, Pixie's fidgeting causes the popcorn to fall, the drink to spill, and Pixie's father hears the malted chocolate balls roll under the seats. Pixie's parents explode in a fit of "movie madness." They pull Pixie out from under the movie chairs as she whines about not getting the malted balls from the floor. Pixie kicks and screams as her parents haul her out to the lobby.

Parents of young children know that everything will be spilled within the first 10 minutes. This is a realistic expectation, particularly for the accident-prone, fidgety ADHD child. As Pixie's case illustrates, ADHD children feel confined to sit in a chair for a long period of time. Pixie's hyperactivity leads to an accident. In addition to spilling things, Pixie was distracted further and went in search of the spilled items.

HYPIE THE HUMMINGBIRD ASKS :

What is Pixie doing now? How do her parents feel now? Why is it important to stay in your seat when at a movie theater?

Dr. Reimers' Remedies: Movie Madness

1. Set the rules before going to the movies (e.g., sit quietly, don't get out of your seat).

2. Instead of having a goal of not spilling food or drinks, redirect the goal toward lengthening the time before things are spilled. This is more realistic and less stressful.

3. Give instructions in a supportive manner. "Please be careful not to spill your drink," instead of "Don't you dare spill your food or drink, or else!"

4. Tell the child that he/she will need to be careful not to spill the food because there needs to be enough for his/her pretend friend. You can even make a game out of feeding the pretend friend.

5. Immediately remove your child from the movie if the child becomes too excited and cannot sit still.

6. Allow frequent breaks, such as a trip to the bathroom, water fountain, or lobby to allow the child to let out energy.

7. Give your child a cue when he/she starts fidgeting or squirming. Seat the child next to you or a peer who sits appropriately.

8. Get "the wiggles" out before you go in to the movie theater. Take a walk, go to a park, play sports, etc. Select a movie that the child is interested in such as action or animated movies.

Other Situations (5) Bowel Accidents

Dr. Reimers Explains: No Holding Back

Buzz is playing outside with his friends. Although he was asked if he had to go to the bathroom, Buzz unexpectedly soiled his pants in the middle of playing. The kids notice an odor, see Buzz tugging uncomfortably at his pants, and they quickly realize what happened. They start calling Buzz "Stinky," cruelly taunting him. Buzz trudges home in shame and his self-esteem takes another plunge when his mother scolds him for having a bowel accident: "How many times have I told you, young man, to go to the bathroom before you go out to play?"

Many young children have problems with bowel and bladder control. Psychological reasons could include anxiety, anger, low self-esteem, control issues, or lack of attention. In addition, young children with ADHD are often reluctant to interrupt their play to find a bathroom. The results can be embarrasing.

Dr. Reimers' Remedies: No Holding Back

1. When the child has a bowel accident, calm down and don't yell or embarrass the child. If you can regain control, that will help your ADHD child regain control.

2. Have the child's pretend friend help with the clean-up. For example, "Here Buzz, you and 'Jakey' are going to throw the dirty clothes in the hamper."

3. Have your child check in with the pretend friend to see if the pretend friend needs to go to the bathroom. This helps the child pay attention to his/her internal body signals.

4. Give your child a star for every day he does not have a bowel accident and allow your child to trade in the stars for rewards.

5. Schedule frequent restroom breaks. Praise other children and the child's pretend friend for going to the bathroom or for taking bathroom breaks.

6. Use logical consequences if the child continues to have bowel accidents. Restrict play opportunities or the amount of time spent at the playground.

7. Give the child a predetermined cue when it is time to take a bathroom break.

8. Check with your child's doctor to see if there is a physiological problem causing the bowel accidents.

9. Talk to the child or his/her pretend friend to see if there are any emotions contributing to the bowel accidents.

Other Situations (6) At a Fast Food Restaurant

HYPIE THE HUMMINGBIRD ASKS :

What is Pixie doing? Why is she making a mess with the ketchup? How does Pixie's mother feel about the mess that Pixie made? Why? What do you think will happen next? Why? How should you behave when you eat out?

Dr. Reimers Explains: Cheeseburger Meltdown

Pixies goes with her mother into a fast food hamburger restaurant. After getting her cheeseburger, Pixie dashes off to get some ketchup. Frustrated by the clogged ketchup pump, she hits it with her fist, knocking it over and getting it all over her hands and clothes. Pixie begins wailing and thrashing when her mother pulls her away from the mess.

Similar to Pixie, her mom is also having an emotional meltdown. She has to deal with many things all at once: cleaning up the mess, cleaning up Pixie, dealing with the scornful stares from others, and managing Pixie's emotional outburst. Exxasperated and mentally drained is how most parents feel when an episode such as this happens.

Unrestrained emotional outbursts, rapid mood changes, and extreme excitability are characteristics of young children and those with ADHD, in particular. Becoming easily frustrated is a major trait of ADHD. This can lead to explosive behavior.

Dr. Reimers' Remedies: Cheeseburger Meltdown

1. When you feel your "meltdown" starting, count to 10, take two deep breaths, and reset your watch, even if it doesn't need resetting. Resetting your watch symbolizes resetting or redirecting your mindset. Remind yourself that this is not a typical child, and the situation needs to be handled calmly.

2. Before going to any public place, review the rules with your child, i.e., hold parent's hand, no running, no touching things without parent's supervision, etc.

3. Choose children's meals that have toys, which help keep the child occupied. If no toys are available, bring one to the restaurant. Use the toy to facilitate imaginative play while eating. The toy could be used as an "eating monster." The child must eat his/her food before the "eating monster" gobbles up all the food.

5. Supervise the child closely. You could have the child assist you in getting ketchup or drinks. The child's imaginary friend can help, too. You can reward the imaginary friend and the child for walking, sitting nicely, and eating all the food.

6. Always expect your child to behave properly at mealtimes, whether at home or at a restaurant. If the child gets out of control, remove the child and go home. The child must understand that eating out is a privilege.

7. Make sure your child knows what the reward will be for appropriate behavior at the restaurant. Be sure to reward the child for good behavior.

Other Situations (7) Losing Things

HYPIE THE HUMMINGBIRD ASKS :

What has happened? Why has Pixie lost some of her belongings? How does her mother feel about Pixie losing things? Why? What do you think will happen next? Why? What can you do so you won't lose things?

Dr. Reimers Explains: Losing Things

Pixie and her mother are going to the park. Since it is cold outside, Pixie's mom dresses her warmly in a hat, scarf, mittens, and overcoat. At the park, Pixie climbs the trees, plays in the sandbox, rides the swing, and runs and jumps everywhere. By the time they return home from the park, Pixie is missing her hat, her scarf, one of her mittens, and one of her shoes.

Parents are always amazed at how their child manages to lose everything, even when closely supervised. Losing things is common for ADHD kids, just as losing tempers can sometimes be for their parents. ADHD children are easily distracted, and they do not pay attention to where they put things. Instead of stopping to watch where they place things, ADHD children are already directing their attention toward the next activity as they absentmindedly drop things and run on. The discipline to put things back in their place requires sustained concentration, which ADHD children typically lack.

Wait, Mommy...
I forgot my mitten!

Great!

HYPIE THE HUMMINGBIRD ASKS :

What is happening now? If you were going out, and did not want to lose something, what would you do? Why is it important to pay attention to your own belongings?

Dr. Reimers' Remedies: Losing Things

1. Before you lose your temper, think "redirect." It does no good to yell at the child. Redirect your energy in a positive way. Have the child retrace her steps.

2. Teach the child the "three-time reminder" technique: Whenever the child puts something down, the child should look at the item, and tell the item to "stay there." The child should repeat the procedure three times for it to stay in the child's memory.

3. Discuss the natural consequences that will occur due to losing items. For example, we won't be able to play at the park if we don't have the things that keep us warm; if you lose this toy, I won't replace it until you can remember where you put things.

4. Have the child's imaginary friend help the child to find the lost item. Reward the child for remembering where he/she has put things.

6. If other children are going with the ADHD child on an outing encourage them to remind the ADHD child to keep track of personal items.

7. Stop periodically to see if the child still has everything.

8. Use something (such as a rubber band around the wrist) to remind the child to keep track of personal items.

9. Set aside some time on regular basis for you to supervise the child to help organize his/her room. Establish a designated place for the child to place items.

Other Situations (8) At the Shopping Mall

HYPIE THE HUMMINGBIRD ASKS :

What is Buzz doing? Why is he bumping other people and climbing on things? How does Buzz's mother feel? How do the other people feel? When you go to the mall, how should you behave? Why?

Dr. Reimers Explains: The Mall Fall

Buzz goes with his mom to the shopping mall. Buzz typically runs ahead of his mom, taking in all the sights of the mall, with his mom chasing after him. Buzz bumps into other shoppers, knocking their bags, stepping on their toes, and nearly knocking over some store displays. Buzz spots a special exhibit of dinosaurs that move and make noises. Before his mom can say no, Buzz has pushed aside some kids, slipped under the rope, and scampered to the top of a 10 foot dinosaur. Mom screams at him to get down. Buzz jumps into the plants, slips into the fish pond, and gets all wet.

Going to the mall with ADHD children doesn't really make a big splash with parents as much as it does for the kids. Because ADHD children are unable to inhibit their impulses, it's not surprising that they would lose control at all, where everythng is exciting, interesting, and stimulating. And with their need for immediate gratification, their overstimulation leads to impulsive, disastrous behavior.

Dr. Reimers' Remedies: The Mall Fall

1. Use the 1-2-3 method to stop behaviors. This means no talking or arguing with the child, and dealing with the child without emotion. If the child's behavior has not changed after three warnings, the child receives a time out.

2. If the child throws a temper tantrum in the mall (such as in front of the candy store) just continue to walk, keeping the child in view. Soon the child will get up and run to where the parents are. Then proceed with a time out. Here are some suggestions about where you can have a time out in the mall:
   a. A bench in the mall.
   b. The corner of a store.
   c. The store's bathroom.
   d. Right where you stand, holding hands.
   e. In the car for a few minutes.

3. Establish rules for behavior in public places. Review them frequently.

4. Reward the child for behaving appropriately in public places. Before going to the mall, for example, tell the child that you'll take him/her to the pet store or to a fast food restaurant if the child can behave nicely.

5. Supervise your child in public places to help the child achieve success. Do not allow your child to go to public places unless the child can follow the rules. Hold the child's hand.

6. Have your child recite the rules to you or to the imaginary friend.

Other Situations (9) On an Airplane

Dr. Reimers Explains: Flying the Unfriendly Skies

Pixie is so excited about going on an airplane to Disneyland. As she explores the items in the pocket seat in front of her, she notices some audio headsets. She takes all the headsets that she can find and ties them into one big knot. When it is time to watch a movie, the flight attendant is shocked, the passengers are angry, mom is mortified, and Pixie is proud. Mom begins yelling at her, the flight attendant begins lecturing her, and the passengers scowl at her. This flight feels anything but friendly to Pixie.

Parents of ADHD children often find themselves feeling embarrassed about the public misbehavior of their child. In a restricted environment, such as riding on an airplane, a restless child has very few outlets for hyperactivity. The child may have difficulty lowering his/her activity level from the hustle and bustle of the airport and waiting room, to a much quieter, smaller airplane cabin. Seeking stimulation, the hyperactive child will try to find things to keep busy. This often leads to trouble.

Dr. Reimers' Remedies: Flying the Unfriendly Skies

1. Put yourself in the child's shoes. How would it feel to be scolded by not just your parents, but also by strangers? Redirect your feelings from those of anger and shame to those of patience and empathy.

2. Before the flight, establish and review the rules for riding on an airplane. You can also review the rules with your child together with the flight attendant.

3. Reward your child for riding on the airplane appropriately.

4. Allow your child to take on the plane any toys, coloring books, and other items that would keep the child's hands busy.

5. Speak to your child's imaginary friend. Ask how the imaginary friend is feeling. Is he/she afraid of flying?

6. Give your child responsibilities while on the airplane (e.g., watching over a younger sibling, looking for other airplanes).

7. Play lots of games such as board travel games, or "I Spy,"

8. Write a contract with your child (e.g.,"I Pixie, will not kick the seat in front of me, pull down the food tray or window blind for the entire trip. When I _____ accomplish this, I will be able to buy a special toy at Disneyland that costs under $10.").

9. Ask the flight attendant if they have any activity kits for child passengers.

Other Situations (10) Birthday Parties

Dr. Reimers Explains: The Birthday Bash

Today is Tommy's birthday. Buzz is one of the guests at the party. One of the highlights of the party is the Pinata. All the children line up in a neat row to put on a blindfold and take their turns at hitting the Pinata with a stick. But Buzz is not joining in with the other children. Instead, Buzz is busy running around Tommy's house, sticking his fingers in the birthday cake, guzzling punch, and gobbling cookies. Finally, one of the children manages to break the Pinata open, scattering candy and little toys all over the ground. Buzz hears the commotion, and by the time he arrives at the scene all the other children have scooped up the candy and prizes. Buzz feels left out and angry. Seeing the stick on the ground, Buzz grabs it and whacks one of the children across the bottom in a fit of anger.

At social gatherings like birthday parties, many children with ADHD often play alone and don't join in on the activities. Despite the fact that the ADHD child doesn't join in, the child can still feel left out and upse. Low frustration tolerance and poor impulse control usually cause the child to act out these negative feelings.

Dr. Reimers' Remedies: The Birthday Bash

1. Keep an eye on the ADHD child at social gatherings, to monitor any possible frustrations and act before any situation escalates out of control. Encourage the ADHD child to verbalize his/her emotions when feeling frustrated.

2. Encourage the ADHD child to participate in social activities so he will not wander off alone.

3. While a game is in progress, talk with the child to keep him focused. Describe the rules, what's going on and coach the child on how to play.

4. Prior to attending any social event (such as a birthday party), describe what the child can expect to see there. You could simulate a birthday party at home to help the child understand the routines, rules or manners that everyone will follow. Another idea you can try is to use a children's video depicting a birthday party to help the child learn what to do.

5. Ask the child why he does not want to participate in parties or other social events. Get the child to talk about his fears, if any. Try to have a familiar friend or older sibling accompany the ADHD child to the party, to help the child feel comfortable and join in.

6. Make it clear to the child that misbehavior at parties or other social events will result in the child being taken home early.

7. Provide controlled opportunities for socialization (e.g., have the child plan a slumber party and invite a friend or two who you know will behave appropriately).

Other Situations (11) Playing with Sticks

HYPIE THE HUMMINGBIRD ASKS :
What happened? Why were Buzz and the boy playing with sticks? How does the boy feel? How would you feel if someone hit you with a stick? What are other ways of using sticks instead of for fighting? What do you think will happen next?

Dr. Reimers Explains: The Pre-School Gladiator

Buzz just loves sticks. He loves the feel of them in his hand. He loves the sounds they make when he hits them against things. And best of all, Buzz likes sticks because they help him feel strong and in charge. Buzz and sticks are inseparable. On a trip to the local park, Buzz finds a sturdy stick, and whacks away at bushes and rocks. He also relishes the sounds the stick makes on the slide and monkey bars. Another boy soon comes along, wielding a stick and challenges Buzz to a sword fight. The two are clashing away like two knights of old. Unfortunately, Buzz takes the duel to a more dangerous level and whacks the boy across the side of his face. The boy runs off screaming.

ADHD children are more prone to higher states of arousal, and this often takes the form of emotional outbursts or aggressive behavior. ADHD children also may have low self-esteem, and thus they compensate by controlling others, often through aggression. Frequently, conflicts build up in stages, but the ADHD child doesn't know how to inhibit his response at each stage before it goes too far.

Dr. Reimers' Remedies: The Pre-School Gladiator

1. Discourage the child from letting out his energy in aggressive ways. Redirect the child toward more calming, constructive activities when you see him starting to act aggressively.

2. Supervise the child to prevent him from becoming overstimulated..

3. Give the child a predetermined cue when he starts to engage in dangerous activities.

4. Have the child play with a friend who does not engage in dangerous activities, such as mock fighting.

5. Point out what he/she did wrong and suggest the appropriate behavior.

6. Provide meaningful activities for the child, so that he will not have any idle time to get into dangerous or rough play.

7. Should the child become overexcited intervene and direct the child to calm down (count to three and take three deep breaths, then repeat).

8. Redirect the child to a more vigorous, but safe activity to expend the child's excess energy.

9. In front of the child, talk with the child's imaginary friend, praising the child for playing appropriately.

Other Situations (12) Misusing Other's Belongings

Dr. Reimers Explains: The Intense Musician

Pixie is visiting a friend's house. Her friend has many toys, among which are some toy musical instruments. Pixie enjoys playing on the toy piano, but soon lets her excitement and curiosity take over. Instead of using her fingers to press the keys of the toy piano, Pixie starts using her fist, banging on the keyboard. Then she finds a toy doll, and uses it to bang the piano keys to hear what kind of sound it would make. Then Pixie uses her feet. After a few minutes, Pixie becomes overexcited and ends up kicking the piano around the room like a soccer ball, hitting her friend.

Children with ADHD can easily become excited when over stimulated. They may get carried away and not show the proper respect for other children's belongings. This behavior may escalate to the point where the child becomes destructive and needs to be removed from the situation to calm down.

Dr. Reimers' Remedies: The Intense Musician

1. Take away any toys or objects the child uses to make noise. Redirect the child to quietly use other toys or belongings.

2. Prior to visiting someone's house, explain to the child the importance of respecting other people's property. Tell her to play gently with other children's toys.

3. Make it clear to the child that if she plays too roughly with other people's belongings, you will take the child home early.

4. Enlist the help of the child's imaginary friend to cue the child when she starts to get too noisy or plays too rough with other people's belongings (e.g., "Hey Pixie, your pretend friend Trixie says that you're getting too loud with that piano.").

5. Use "what if" scenarios to help the child understand and empathize with other people's feelings (e.g.,"Pixie, how would you feel if your friend broke your favorite dolly? You would feel sad, right? Well, Tracy feels the same way when you kicked her toy piano."). Role play with the child, demonstrating appropriate ways to use things.

7. Invite a friend over to play, and explain how nicely that friend plays with toys. Encourage the child to play in the same considerate manner when she goes to play at the friend's house someday.

8. Make a contract with the child (e.g.,"I, Pixie, will play nicely with Tracy's things when I go to play at her house today. If I do, Mommy will take me out for an ice cream cone later.").

Other Situations (13) At the Swimming Pool

Dr. Reimers Explains: 20,000 Bobs Under the Sea

Pixie is taking tiny tot swim lessons at a public pool, and is waiting in the water for her turn to practice swimming with the instructor. Pixie soon gets bored with waiting, and she starts to put her head under the water to see how things look under water. As she dunks under the water, she lets go of the pool side, and bobs a couple of times, enjoying the sensation of floating, even though she cannot swim. Then Pixie frantically splashes to grab the side of the pool again. The instructor sees Pixie dangerously bobbing around without holding onto the edge of the pool, and warns Pixie to hold onto the edge and wait her turn. But Pixie doesn't listen, and after three more warnings, the instructor sends Pixie out of the pool to take some time out. Pixie shivers in the air, sitting in a puddle, wondering what the fuss was all about.

ADHD children are natural thrill-seekers and their urge to explore often overpowers any concerns for their own safety or any motivation to follow rules. It is not that ADHD children want to hurt themselves; they simply do not think about dangerous consequences. Their impulsivity causes them to live in the moment.

Great!

HYPIE THE HUMMINGBIRD ASKS :

What is happening now? Is Pixie being safe at the pool? How does her teacher feel now? Why? When you are at the pool, what can you do to be safe? What are some things you should not do at a swimming pool?

Dr. Reimers' Remedies: 20,000 Bobs under the Sea

1. Prior to going to a swimming pool, review the safety rules. Make it clear that you will remove the child from the pool if the child doesn't follow the rules. Offer a reward if the child behaves appropriately.

2. When the child misbehaves in the pool, have the child take a time-out and point out what she was doing wrong, and discuss the appropriate behavior. If swim class rules allow parents to be near the pool side with the children, maintain close supervision of the child at all times. Otherwise, at least maintain visual contact.

4. Identify another child who obeys the pool rules, and encourage your ADHD child to imitate that child.

5. Make a contract with your child (e.g., "I, Pixie, will obey the safety rules of the pool. If I follow the rules, I can go to the pool an extra day.").

6. Coach the child to ask herself questions when she starts to misbehave (e.g.,"What am I doing right now?" "What should I be doing?""What will happen if I don't obey the rules?").

7. While the child waits her turn with the instructor, keep her busy by having her practice kicking under water, blowing bubbles, bobbing up and down while holding on the side of the pool, etc.

8. Whether in or out of the pool, have the child rehearse the pool safety rules with her imaginary friend.

Other Situations (14) Misinterpreting Social Cues

Dr. Reimers Explains: The Social Misinterpreter

Buzz sees some of his friends at the park. He approaches them to join in on their game of tag. But the kids, knowing that Buzz always plays too rough, avoid him, and move away from him. They frown at Buzz, and tell him to "get lost," but Buzz doesn't take the hint. Buzz keeps trying to play tag with the kids. Exasperated, the children finally go to play somewhere else, leaving Buzz behind, and upset. Buzz can't understand; all he wanted to do was play with them.

Many ADHD children lack basic social skills to interact positively with others, and are often oblivious to social cues. They have difficulty discerning the changes in the tone of voice or body language of peers that imply that the child's behavior is irritating them. When the child's impulsivity is added to the equation, the problem is compounded, often annoying the child's peers and resulting in rejection. Any unfavorable reputation that the ADHD child has among his peers may continue long after the child has changed his behavior.

Dr. Reimers' Remedies: The Social Misinterpreter

1. Teach the child the basic skill of apologizing. Coach your child on how to admit responsibility, acknowledge the feelings of others, and make amends.

2. Using role playing, help the child think about how he can do things differently in various social situations, to avoid repeating the same mistakes.

3. To help your child learn non-verbal body language, look through a magazine together, and discuss the facial gestures of people. Ask your child to guess what each person may be thinking or feeling, and help the child identify basic expressions and postures.

4. Help your child cultivate basic friendship skills (e.g., talk to people rather than stay silent, do what they want to do, smile, exchange or respond to greetings, invite someone to play with you).

5. Rehearse various tones of voice or manners of speaking with the child, to help him distinguish between angry, fearful, teasing, happy or other vocal tones.

6. Teach the child to think empathetically (e.g., "How would you feel if....?").

7. Help the child practice to verbalize feelings, using "when you...I...." statements (e.g., "When you frown at me, I don't know why.").

8. Practice with the child, to help him/her label emotions correctly (e.g., when someone smiles at the child, help the child understand that the person isn't making fun of the him, but is being friendly).

Other Situations (15) Getting Lost at the Store

Dr. Reimers Explains: Lost & Found

Pixie and her mother visit a department store during a big clearance sale. Pixie's excitement grows with the hectic environment of the store, as shoppers crowd the aisles, and clerks rush to and fro. Pixie's mother tells her to hold onto her hand, so she wont get lost. But Pixie isn't in the mood for holding hands. There is so much to see and touch at the department store, and so Pixie lets go of her mother's hand and runs ahead to look at jewelry displays and clothes. Amid the bustling crowd, it doesn't take long for Pixie to get lost. With her mother nowhere in sight, Pixie starts crying. She wonders how she could lose her mother after only a few seconds. After a few minutes, a clerk notices Pixie and makes an announcement over the intercom, and Pixie is reunited with her worried mother.

Remember that when you take an easily distractible child to a store or shopping mall, you cannot always expect the child to stay next to you. Any motivation to obey and stay close by is tuned out by the tremendous urge to see and touch everything. Often a child with ADHD will impulsively run ahead or lag behind, oblivious to the danger of being separated from parents.

Dr. Reimers' Remedies: Lost & Found

1. Before going to a store or shopping mall, talk with the child about the importance of holding hands or staying close by. Review the rules about what to do if the child gets lost (e.g., tell a clerk that your are lost, stay in one place and wait, be able to tell one's own name and the parent's names).

2. To keep your child from running ahead of you or lagging behind, make a verbal contract, promising some reward if the child can stay within arm's reach of you.

3. If the child does not want to hold your hand, you and the child can hold onto a purse or shopping bag together, or have the child hold onto part of a shopping cart or baby carriage. You can even allow the child to help push the shopping cart.

4. Assign the child some responsibilities to keep her nearby. At the grocery store, for example, your child can help select items off the shelves, hold onto the shopping list, help check off items on the shopping list, count-off, weigh or otherwise measure items as you put them into the shopping cart.

5. Don't rush! Allow yourself enough time to go slowly through the store, taking time to stop and talk about items that catch your child's attention.

6. Use time-outs to reinforce the rules if the child disobeys intentionally.

7. Keep the child nearby and focused by engaging her in a game of "I Spy," pointing out colors or shapes (e.g.,"I Spy with my little eye something...RED! Guess what it is?").

CHAPTER 7

Assessment of ADHD

Is a Professional Evaluation Necessary?

Like many parents of ADHD children, you may have suspected early on that something wasn't quite right about your child's behavior. As an infant he may have been temperamental, hard to soothe, or difficult to put asleep. As he learned to crawl and eventually walk, he may have been hyperactive, easily distracted, and more emotional than other children the same age. He may have shown a lack of judgment before acting, or acted aggressively. You probably tried all you could to correct his misbehavior, but nothing seemed to work.

Your child's problems could also have been brought to your attention by his teacher or other school staff. He may have been disruptive in class, had few friends, and had difficulty staying on task in his classroom activities.

It is important to take constructive action if you think your child is having a problem. If you think there could be a problem with ADHD, request a professional evaluation. Look for the following signs:

- Your child consistently displays hyperactivity, inattentiveness, or impulsiveness for a prolonged period.

- Other parents tell you about your child's poor self-control.
- Much of your time and energy is spent managing your child's behavior and safety.
- Your child cannot keep his hands to himself. He touches people and things too much.
- Your child seems unusually accident-prone, or is a risk taker.
- Other children do not want to play with your child because of his hyperactivity, aggressiveness, or misbehavior.
- Your child's teacher or day care provider tells you that your child has been having major behavioral problems for several months.
- Your child seems unable to make friends or sustain friendships with other children. He tends to play with younger children.
- You are frequently losing your temper with your child, or feeling fatigued, frustrated, or depressed about your child's behavior.
- Your child is very impatient, wants everything now, and doesn't take "no" for an answer.
- Your child understands the rules for home and school, yet seems unable to obey them.

If you experience any of these symptoms, you should consider having your child assessed for ADHD by the school or by a qualified professional. For some parents, the decision to seek a professional evaluation for their child is not an easy one. Rest assured, however, that the earlier ADHD is diagnosed, the sooner you can treat your child and begin to find solutions to the behavior problems that may have dominated your life.

Requesting an Assessment Through Your School

Your child's school should be able to provide you with information to help you set up an assessment for your child through your local school district. Assessment services for children suspected of having special needs are covered and paid for under the Individuals with Disabilities in Education Act (IDEA) and Section 504 of the Rehabilitation Act of 1973. These laws guarantee a free, appropriate, public education to children with disabilities, including ADHD.

What is Included in the Assessment of ADHD?

The Evaluation Process
This will look at the whole child and will include information on the child's total environment.

- The parent interview with the professional is usually the starting point for most evaluations. During this initial interview parents will be asked to provide information about the presenting problems leading to seek professional help. The interviewer will ask questions about the child's developmental history including any medical, social, or emotional difficulties. A detailed school history will generally be taken even if the child has only attended preschool or the primary grades. Additional information about the family will be obtained to determine whether ADHD is/was present in other family members. During this interview the professional will most likely determine what additional steps to take in the evaluation process.

- The professional will want to observe the child one or more times. This observation may take place at the home, at school, or in the professional's office. The child may or may not be interviewed during this observation. Data will be collected on how the child behaves in natural settings (home, school, or play) or how the child manages structured and unstructured tasks presented by the interviewer or others.

- The professional and the parents meet with the child's teacher(s) and other school staff to gather information regarding the child's behavior in the classroom. Cumulative records may be examined and other assessment data may be reviewed.

- There will be a review of the child's medical history and consultation with other health professionals familiar with the child. A medical examination may be necessary to rule out any medical problems which could cause symptoms of ADHD.

- Parents and teachers will be asked to complete one or more rating scales to characterize patterns of the child's behavior at home, in school, and in other settings. More than one type of rating scale may be used to obtain several different views of the child.

- Psychological testing of the child may be important to determine intellectual ability and to look for possible learning disabilities. Testing for emotional difficulties may also be done to check for depression, anxiety or other factors that can influence the child's behavior.

- After completing the assessment, the professional will meet with the parents and teacher(s) to report the findings.

Who is Involved?

A multidisciplinary team should be involved in performing the evaluation. The following professionals may be included.
- Private or school psychologist
- Speech and language pathologist
- Occupational therapist
- Physical therapist and/or adaptive physical education therapist
- Medical specialist(s)
- Educational diagnostician(s)
- Classroom teacher(s)
- Others

Which Areas are Tested?

These professionals will observe your child and some may administer tests that examine the child's:
- speech and language functioning
- personality and adaptive behavior patterns
- academic achievement
- cognitive functioning (intelligence)
- perceptual functioning (i.e., memory, motor coordination, etc.)
- attention span and impulse control

As you consider the assessment options for your child, there are some important questions you should consider. In Appendix C you will find a list of questions that have been prepared by the Parents Educational Resource Center (P.E.R.C.) of San Mateo, California, to help guide parents before, during, and after the assessment process.

Which Tests are Used to Assess ADHD?

Contrary to what you would expect, there is no single test that can diagnose ADHD. The professional has several assessment tools at his or her disposal to test your child for ADHD. Remember that ADHD is a complicated disorder with intertwining symptoms. Some of these symptoms may be more subtle than others, and only proper testing using several assessment tools may help identify them. While there are many tests available, we have selected the more popular testing instruments for younger children.

Intelligence Tests
- Wechsler Preschool and Primary Scale of Intelligence-III (WPPSI-III)
- Stanford-Binet Intelligence Scale (5th Edition)
- Pictorial Test of Intelligence (PTI)
- McCarthy Scales of Children's Abilities
- Kaufman Assessment Battery for Children (K-ABC)
- Woodcock-Johnson III Tests of Cognitive Abilities

Rating Scales
- Vineland Adaptive Behavioral Scales
- Homes Situations Questionnaire
- Child Behavioral Checklist (CBCL)
- Conners Parent Rating Scale-Revised
- Conners Teacher Rating Scale-Revised
- Behavior Assessment System for Children
- Child Behavior Checklist
- Vanderebilt Assessment Scale

Continuous Performance Tests
- Test of Variables of Attention (TOVA)
- Conners' Continuous Performance Test
- Gordon Diagnostic System
- Integrated Visual and Auditory Continuous Performance Test (IVA)

Weschler Preschool and Primary Scale of Intelligence-Revised (WPPSI-III)

This test consists of 14 subtests that measure Verbal IQ ,Performcance IQ, Processing Speed and Fu ll Scale IQ for ages four to seven years. It takes about one hour and a half hours to administer. It is one of the best intelligence tests available.

Stanford-Binet Intelligence Scale (5th Edition)

This test consists of subtests grouped into five factors measuring: fluid reasoning, knowledge, quantitative processing, visual-spatial processing, and working memory It takes approximately two hours to administer and can be used with children as yoiung as two years.

Pictorial Test of Intelligence (PTI)

This test contains six subtests: picture vocabulary, form discrimination, information and comprehension, similarities, size and number, and immediate recall. The PTI was designed for children ages three to eight. It takes about 45 minutes to administer. It serves as a supplementary nonverbal measure of learning aptitude for young children with motor and speech handicaps.

McCarthy Scales of Children's Abilities

This test is comprised of eighteen tests grouped into six scales: verbal, perceptual/performance, quantitative, memory, motor, and general cognitive. It is used for children ages 2 1/2 to 8 1/2. It provides a general cognitive index, and it takes about one hour to administer. It is a useful test for ADHD children because it measures the child's fine and gross motor ability, memory, and general intelligence. However, since the general cognitive index is not as thorough, it is not necessarily comparable with those scores obtained on other intelligence tests. An added advantage is that the test is enjoyable for the child to take.

Kaufman Assessment Battery for Children (K-ABC)

This test is designed to assess intelligence and achievement. It is appropriate for children ages 2 1/2 to 12 1/2. It takes 45-75 minutes to administer. The test is limited because it fails to include a composite verbal cognitive score. It is useful when a nonverbal measure of ability is needed. It is also excellent for the diagnosis of learning disabilities.

Woodcock-Johnson Psycho-Educational Battery (Third Edition)

This test contains tests that cover assessment of cognitive ability, achievement, and interest. It is for ages three to adult. Not all areas are tested at every age. It takes two hours to administer.

Vineland Adaptive Behavioral Scales (VABS)

This is a behavior rating scale that measures four areas of adaptive behavior (communication, daily living skills, socialization, and motor skills) and one general area of maladaptive behavior. It is for ages newborn to adult, and takes about 60-90 minutes to administer. Respondent is either the parent, teacher, or someone who is familiar with the child.

Home Situations Questionnaire

This questionnaire lists 16 different situations at home. The parents indicate if this situation is a problem (yes/no), and if yes, how severe it is on a scale of one to nine. If 50% or more of the items are checked "yes," ADHD may could be considered.

Child Behavioral Checklist (CBCL)

This is a behavioral checklist that provides a profile of behavioral problems and social competence. For ages two to 16. It takes approximately 30-40 minutes to administer. The respondent is the parent.

Conners' Rating Scale-Revised (Parent Versions)

These are behavioral checklists for the parent to fill out, either in a long version (consisting of 80 items) or a short version (27 items) including scales for categories like oppositional behavior, cognitive problems, hyperactivity-impulsivity, anxious-shy, perfectionism, DSM-IV symptoms, etc. This rating scale is suitable for ages 3 to 17. It takes about 20 to 40 minutes to administer. This is one of the most popular scales used for measuring ADHD symptoms from a parent's perspective.

Conners' Rating Scale Revised (Teacher Versions)

These are behavioral checklists for the teacher to fill out, either in a long version (consisting of 59 items) or a short version (28 items). The long version includes scales for categories like oppositional behavior, cognitive problems, hyperactivity-impulsivity, anxious-shy, perfectionism, DSM-IV symptoms, etc. It takes about 30 minutes to administer. This is one of the most popular scales used for measuring ADHD symptoms in the classroom setting.

Attention-Deficit/Hyperactivity Disorder Test (ADHDT)

Designed by James E. Gilliam for use in schools and clinics, it is easily completed by teachers, parents or others. Appropriate for ages 3 to 23, and takes 5 to 10 minutes to administer. It is based on the DSM-IV symptom criteria (described in chapter 2), and measures for hyperactivity, impulsivity and inattention.

Test of Variables of Attention (TOVA®)

The TOVA is a continuous performance test that requires the test taker to attend to one of two symbols appearing very briefly on a computer screen. The subject must press a switch when one symbol (a square with a hole at the top) appears and not when another (a square with a hole at the bottom) appears. The test is introduced as the "paying attention game" and most children seem to have no difficulty understanding the directions. The TOVA measures inattention, impulsivity, response time (a measure of speed of processing information), and variability (a measure of consistency).

Conners' Continuous Performance Test®

Another continuous performance test that requires the test taker to attend to a series of letters presented on a screen. The subject must respond to these letters which vary in sequence and rate of presentation. Similar to other continuous performance tests, this one measures speed of responding, errors resulting from inattention, errors resulting from impulsivity, and other variables.

Gordon Diagnostic System®

This continuous performance test has been extensively standardized and presents several tasks to the test-taker which measure impulsivity, inattention, and response inhibition.

Integrated Visual and Auditory Continuous Performance Test (IVA®)

This continuous performance test is unique in that it combines visual and auditory stimuli to measure inattention and impulsivity. The subject is instructed to click the mouse only when he or she sees or hears a "1" and not to click when he or she sees or hears a "2."

The Individualized Education Program (IEP)

Once your child has been evaluated, the child study team at school may review the results to determine if your child is eligible to receive any special programs or services at school. If it is determined that the child has a disability (e.g., ADHD) and the disability adversely affects educational performance, the child may be eligible to receive special education services under IDEA. If so determined, the school will prepare an Individualized Education Program (IEP) designed to specifically meet the child's needs. The IEP specifies the services and programs that the child will receive as a result of his/her disability.

What is Included in an IEP?

An IEP must include the following:

1. A statement of the child's present level of educational performance, based on the assessment.
2. Annual goals and measurable short-term objectives.
3. A listing of the special education and related services provided to the child.
4. A statement of the extent of participation in regular education programs.
5. The date services are to begin and the anticipated duration of those services.
6. Appropriate procedures for evaluating short-term objectives on at least an annual basis.
7. The signatures of all participants, along with their titles. All participants must also individually date the IEP.
8. The amount of time the child will be given related services (e.g., speech therapy).
9. Any special considerations or arrangements needed by the child.
10. Any special materials or equipment the child will use.
11. Communication strategies established between the parents and the professionals who will work with the child.

Who is on the IEP Team?

The IEP team is the group of individuals that plan and write the IEP. The IEP team should consist of the following people:

1. The child's parents.
2. The principal or special education director for the school district, who is authorized to commit the necessary funding for the child's educational and related services.
3. The child's teacher(s).
4. A member of the evaluation team who is knowledgeable about the evaluation procedures and outcomes and who has knowledge of the child's ADHD (such as the school counselor, school psychologist, or private practice psychologist).
5. Anyone invited to attend the IEP meeting by the child's parents. This could be a friend or a relative, a case manager or anyone else the parents wish to invite for moral support or as another advocate for the child.

The IEP Meeting

The IEP meeting is a conference in which members of the IEP team get together to develop or review the IEP. This meeting can be called by a parent, support staff or by school staff at any time, and is requested in writing. The purpose of the IEP meeting is to:

1. Review the records and assessments.
2. Discuss the strengths and needs of the child.
3. Formulate goals and objectives.
4. Identify an appropriate program for the child's needs, which includes the designated instructional services (such as speech therapy, etc.) in order for the child to benefit from his primary program.

At the IEP meeting, goals and objectives are proposed, modified or deleted until everyone (especially the parents) feel comfortable with them. Everyone in the meeting is given the opportunity to give input. The parents need to share their special insight about the child, and voice their concerns. Services for the child should be determined by what is needed, not by what is available. Cost is never an issue and should not be mentioned.

Most often the IEP meeting is a positive experience for all involved. Sometimes there are differences of opinion, but the parents must stand up for what they believe is best for the child. If the team members know that the parents understand their legal rights and if the parents' views are well thought out and presented with accurate information, the team members are more likely to listen.

When the parents and the other members of the IEP team have completed developing and writing the IEP, the parents will be asked to sign it. Even if the parents agree with the IEP, they do not have to sign it at the meeting. The parents can take the IEP home and take more time to review it. Once the parents feel comfortable with it and sign it, the necessary actions will be taken to implement the child's individualized educational program.

Rejecting the IEP

If you do not feel comfortable with the completed IEP, you need to reject it. Do not sign it.

You will need to contact the school principal, special education director or program manager and state your intention of rejecting the IEP. Tell him or her your concerns, including finding a way to reach an agreement without having to go to mediation or due process.

By verbalizing your intentions of rejection, you give the school personnel the opportunity to rethink their stand. As they come to understand your commitment, they may back down to avoid having to file a Formal Rejection of IEP to the State Department of Education. If you still cannot reach any kind of resolution, then you must formally reject the IEP in writing.

On the IEP form, there is a line which states, "I do not accept the educational program." There is a box to check and a place for your signature and date. There is also room to write comments, if you wish. Make sure that you keep a full copy of the rejected IEP, including the page indicating your rejection.

Section 504 of The Rehabilitation Act of 1973

Your child may be found to have a disability which does not adversely affect educational performance and make him eligible for special education, but which does require that accommodations be made in the regular classroom. Such accommodations ensure that the child has access to a free, appropriate education. The school may prepare a 504 Plan spelling out the accommodations the teacher will make in the regular classroom to assist your child. Such accommodations may include: preferential seating, a behavior plan, home notes, closer supervision, regular consultation with parents or doctors, shorter lessons, social skills training, etc.

Become an Empowered Parent

Parents of children with special needs such as ADHD must become empowered to help their child in school and in partnership with health care professionals in their community.

Empowered parents learn about the responsiblities schools have to provide appropriate educational services to disabled children. Empowered parents become familiar with community resources—public and private. Empowered parents read about current issues in ADHD, methods of treatment, behavior management programs, etc. They are prepared to meet the different challenges ADHD presents as their child grows older or symptoms worsen.

As you become an empowered parent you will establish a link between health care professionals and educators to coordinate services each provides to your child and to ensure that treatment progresses smoothly.

CHAPTER 8

Treatment of ADHD

Medication

Stimulant medications have been used to treat hyperactive children since 1937. Such medications are extremely effective. Over 70 percent of children who take stimulants improve in terms of hyperactivity, impulsivity, and attention span. When other comorbid disorders associated with ADHD are also treated, closer to 85 to 90 percent of children show improvement with a combination of two or three different medications.

There have been hundreds of controlled studies of stimulant medication and ADHD. The results of such studies are incontrovertible. For the short-term, at least, stimulant medication reduces motor overactivity and cognitive overactivity, decreases impulsivity and distractibility, and improves self-control. In addition, improvements in fine and gross motor coordination have been noted, organizational skills, and short-term memory as well. Social relationships improve as stimulant medication may reduce aggressiveness and increase pro-social behaviors in children with ADHD.

Unfortunately, stimulant medications do not have a significant effect on any existing learning disabilities. Children with language-based learning problems will not be helped dramatically by stimulants. However, such medications do assist children whose academic performance (work completion, work accuracy, etc.) has been affected by their ADHD. In such cases, it is not unusual for grades to improve from one to two grade points. Furthermore, improved attention, cognitive functioning, motivation, mental energy, and perseverance help the child to be more cooperative and responsive to other remedial education efforts.

Parents of young children with ADHD are usually concerned about behavior in addition to learning in school. Frequently, the child's behavior problems and the social ramifications of such problems are quite significant. When non-medical interventions fail to provide improvement, many parents of young children with ADHD consider medication as an option. Children as young as two years of age are being treated successfully with stimulant medications.

If you consider medication to help treat your child's ADHD, you must weigh the benefits against the risks (side effects). You must also consider how long each day you want your child placed on medication. Some parents choose to have their child on medication during school hours alone. However, if medication is only used during school hours, the child may continue to have problems with family at home or with peers after school.

I always encourage parents to work closely with their young child before they try medication. If problems with hyperactivity, impulsivity, and inattention do not show improvement then medication should be considered. Consult with a physician or therapist trained in the use of these medications to obtain an accurate picture of what can be accomplished. Ultimately, the choice is yours to make.

Even with correct information, your decision to place your child on medication will still spark controversy with family, friends, and others. You will get raised eyebrows, frowns of disapproval, doubts, and even outright criticism when people hear that you are giving your young child medication. Parents sometimes hear the following remarks.

- Aren't you worried that your child is going to get hooked on those drugs?
- She's too young to be on drugs.
- Your child won't learn to be responsible for his own behavior if he's drugged all the time.
- She might grow up to be a drug addict if you put her on drugs now.
- Using drugs is mind control.
- Your child will be like a zombie while she's on medication.
- Medication will cover up your child's real personality.

Commonly Asked Questions about Medication for ADHD

None of these concerns are consistent with the facts learned from over 50 years of treating children with ADHD with medication. When properly prescribed, used, and monitored, medications to control ADHD behavior are generally safe and not addictive. Let's discuss these misperceptions about ADHD medication so that you can deal confidently, reso-

lutely, and effectively with the criticisms you may encounter.

Q. Do medications for ADHD cause addiction?

A. While there have been reports of abuse of stimulant medication, these are not widespread. Certainly, young children taking stimulants are not at risk for abuse or addiction.

Q. Will ADHD medications prevent the child from learning responsible behavior?

A. Again, the answer is no. These drugs help increase a child's focus and persistence in completing tasks. In school-age children they reduce impulsivity, hyperactivity and distractibility so the child can concentrate on working hard to improve behavior and academic performance.

Q. Will the use of ADHD medications lead to future drug use and addiction?

A. Years of research have shown that there is no proof that children treated with stimulant medications develop any kind of craving for drugs later on in life as a result of taking these medications. In fact, the use of stimulants to treat ADHD in children may lower the risk for future substance abuse.

Q. Will ADHD medication turn your child into a drugged-out zombie? Is it mind control?

A. At proper dosage levels, ADHD children do not experience any slowdown in their mental abilities. A properly medicated ADHD child will have strengthened capacity for independent thinking and creativity, and will display more thoughtfulness.

Q. Will ADHD medication mask your child's real personality?

A. Children taking medication for ADHD symptoms may interact differently with others. They will generally be more calm and less excitable. They may exhibit less spontaneity in their behavior. They will usually get along better with others. They will show more persistence on tasks and stay more focused. You may see some changes in what you regard as "personality characteristics" while the child is on medication, but these changes are not permanent.

When you observe ADHD children who are on successful medication treatment programs combined with effective behavioral training, you will notice that they have improved in their school work, they get along with other kids, they feel better about themselves by being in control, and they get into trouble less often.

Types of Medications Used to Treat ADHD

If a decision is made to place the child on medication, you need to discuss with your health care provider the different options available. Medications used to treat ADHD symptoms can be classified into three groups by their function:

- The primary attention-enhancing stimulant medications (AdderallXR®, Ritalin,®, Ritalin LA®, Focalin® and Focalin XR®, Concerta®, and Metadate CD®)

- The broader spectrum, antidepressant medications with both attention-enhancing plus mood and temper-improving effects(Strattera®,Tofranil,®Norpramine,® Wellbutrin,® and Effexor®).

* The medications that down-regulate over-arousal, hyper-alertness, hyper-vigilance, as well as improve frustration tolerance

and patience (Catapres® and Tenex®).

It is important to point out that, while these drugs are commonly prescribed for children with ADHD and/or other emotional disorders, the safety of these drugs has not been entirely established for children under the age of six years. Therefore, it is our recommendation that you consult with your physician before placing your ADHD child on medication. (For your further reference, in the appendix of this book we have compiled lists of helpful questions to ask physicians/therapists concerning treatments and medications.)

On the following page is a summary chart of commonly-used ADHD medications, grouped by their functions and listing their important characteristics.

You might wonder why stimulants are used to make a hyperactive child calm down. In his book, *Helping Your Hyperactive/Attention Deficit Child*, John Taylor points out that these drugs stimulate the child's 'brake' pedal, whereas without medication, the child is all 'gas' pedal, They do not slow down everything a child does. Instead, they allow a child to do a more efficient job of choosing what to say or do. They also increase the child's ability to solve problems and learn.

The standard procedure is to try different medications, one at a time, until an effective treatment program is established. Work closely with your doctor or therapist to monitor your child's behavior while on and off medication. Keeping a careful record of any side-effects is also important. In Appendix C is a chart you can use to monitor your child's medication treatment.

Also do not forget that your child has normal fluctuations in mood, likes and dislikes and energy level. Medication treatment will help control the child's hyperactivity, impulsivity, distractibility and depression, but it is not a cure for emotional/psychological problems. You will still need to work with the child to develop good self-esteem, good habits, social skills and

(A) THE PRIMARY ATTENTION-ENHANCING MEDICATIONS

DRUG	FORM	DURATION	SIDE EFFECTS	PROS	COMMENTS
RITALIN® Methylphenidate	5 mg, 10 mg, 20 mg tablets	about 3-5 hours	Insomnia, decreased appetite, weight loss, headache, stomachache, irritability	Works quickly (within 30-60 min). Good safety record. Ritalin LA can be sprinkled on applesauce.	Use cautiously with patients with anxiety, motor tics, or Tourette's.
RITALIN LA® Methylphenidate	20, 30, 40 mg capsules	about 8 hours			
CONCERTA® Methylphenidate	18 mg, 27 mg, 36 mg, 54 mg tablets	about 10-14 hours	Insomnia, decreased appetite, weight loss, headache, stomachache, irritability.	Works quickly (within 30-60 min). Good safety record. Given once a day.	Use cautiously with patients with anxiety, motor tics, or Tourette's.
METADATE CD® Methylphenidate	20 mg capsule	about 8 hours	Insomnia, decreased appetite, weight loss, headache, stomachache, irritability.	Works quickly (within 30-60 min). Good safety record.	Use cautiously with patients with anxiety, motor tics, or Tourette's.
FOCALIN® FOCALIN XR® Methylphenidate	2.5 mg, 5 mg, 10 mg 5 mg, 10 mg, 20 mg	about 3-5 hours about 8 hours	Insomnia, decreased appetite, weight loss, headache, stomachache, irritability.	Works quickly (within 30-60 min). Good safety record.	Use cautiously with patients with anxiety, motor tics, or Tourette's.
ADDERALL XR® Amphetamine compounds	5 mg, 10 mg, 15 mg, 20 mg, 25 mg, 30 mg tablets	about 10-12 hours	Insomnia, decreased appetite, weight loss, headache, stomachache, irritability	Works quickly (within 30-60 min). Good safety record. Can be sprinkled on applesauce. Once a day.	Use cautiously with patients with anxiety, motor tics, or Tourette's.

B) THE BROADER SPECTRUM MEDICATIONS WITH BOTH ATTENTION-ENHANCING PLUS MOOD AND TEMPER IMPROVING EFFECTS

DRUG	FORM	DURATION	SIDE EFFECTS	PROS	COMMENTS
STRATTERA® Atomxetine	10 mg, 18 mg, 25 mg, 40 mg, 60 mg capsules	all day	In children-decreased appetite, GI upset (can be reduced iftaken with food), sedation, lightheadedness	Works within a few days to two weeks. Can be taken once a day for all day duration.	Use cautiously in patients with hypertension, tachycardia or cardiovascular disease
NORPRAMIN® Desipramine TOFRANIL® Imipramine	10, 25, 50, 75, 100 150 mg tablets 10, 25, 50, 75, 100, 150 mg tablets and capsules	12-24 hours	Dry mouth, decreased appetite, headache, stomachache, dizziness, constipation, mild tachycardia	Helpful for ADHD patients with co-morbid depression or anxiety; lasts throughout the day.	Not recommended for children under 12 yrs. May take 2-4 wks to work;Baseline ECG may be needed.
EFFEXOR® Venlafaxine	25, 37.5, 50, 75 mg tablets; 37.5, 75, 150 mg extended-release tablets	in 4 to 7 days level in bloodstream lasts up to 48 hours	Headache, nausea, sleepiness, dry mouth, dizziness, insomnia	Considered safest when there is a co-existent cardiovascular problem	May be recommended if mood swings and irritability are co-existent

(C) MEDICATIONS THAT DOWN-REGULATE OVERAROUSAL, HYPER-ALERTNESS, HYPER-VIGILANCE, AND IMPROVE FRUSTRATION TOLERANCE & PATIENCE

DRUG	FORM	DURATION	SIDE EFFECTS	PROS	COMMENTS
CATAPRES® Clonidine	.1mg .2mg .3mg tablets; TTS-1, TTS-2, TTS-3 skin patches	3-6 hours for tablets; 5 days for the skin patch	Sleepiness, hypertension, headache, dizziness, nausea, dry mouth, localized skin reactions with patch	Helpful for ADHD patients with co-morbid tic disorder or severe hyperactivity and/or aggression	Sudden discontinuation could result in rebound hypertension
TENEX® Guanfacine	1mg tablet	up to 4 hours	Dry mouth, sleepiness, dizziness, constipation, fatigue, headache, insomnia	Improves frustration tolerance and impulsivity. Once-a-day dosing	Too high a dose can cause drowsiness and dizziness; Also chance of rebound hypertension

This is not a complete list of medications for treating ADHD. Consult with your physician about your child's specific medication requirements.

practice good behavior. Working with a therapist or other helping professional is highly recommended to deal with the child's emotional side. A multifaceted approach, consisting of a balance of social and emotional therapy, school adjustment and medication treatment, is the most effective approach for helping a child with ADHD.

Counseling

It would be a mistake to conclude that once your child starts medication, his problems will be over. Not only does medication require close monitoring and adjustment, other needs of the child (psychological, academic, social) and the family need to be addressed.

Even when medicated, the ADHD child may still need behavior management training, or may need help with his aggression, oppositional defiant behavior, conduct disturbances, academic difficulties, low self-esteem, depression, and poor peer relationships. One or both parents may need to seek help to deal with their emotional problems. Parents may need to enter couples therapy, the child may need to have individual therapy. Sometimes the entire family may benefit from family therapy.

The counselor you work with may be a psychologist, social worker, marriage and family therapist, mental health counselor, child and adolescent psychiatrist or a member of some other helping profession. The primary goals of the counselor are to assist in diagnosing and treating problem areas and to help your family counter the stresses ADHD poses to your child and family. The services of a counselor or other mental health professional are more effective if sought early.

For the very young child with ADHD individual therapy may not be necessary. However, as the child gets older, therapy can be helpful. The therapist and child can work together to solve problems with behavior, socialization, or family and academic difficulties. Supportive individual therapy may help improve self-esteem and may assist in uncovering other difficulties the child may be experiencing.

If needed, social skills training for the child may be recommended. This may involve individual or small group training in such skills as sharing, cooperative play, initiating and maintaining conversations, understanding others feelings and nonverbal cues, etc. Role playing and practicing may help the child internalize the good behaviors and social skills learned.

Parents may need help dealing with stresses resulting from raising a child with ADHD. Parents play a very important role in advocating for their child with schools and other professionals and agencies. Advocacy training may be a useful part of the counseling process along with general information about ADHD.

Sometimes the entire family is stressed and dysfunctional. In such cases, family therapy may be considered. Family therapy may help family members modify expectations of the ADHD child. Problems with siblings can be dealt with so that they can help the parents work with the ADHD child.

Do your best to have a smooth working relationship between the counselor and your child and between the counselor and yourself. Provide the counselor with your notes on your child's behavior, your interactions with your child, your feelings as a parent, records of medication monitoring, and any other helpful information. Have your questions ready. Take notes. Be straightforward and honest and do not camouflage your problems. Do not be afraid to reveal something you do not understand. Ask for written summaries about therapy sessions for your own records. All of this will foster a respectful, cooperative partnership with your counselor.

Herbal Treatments

There are claims that various herbs, minerals and extracts have beneficial effects on ADHD behavior, without the side effects of some of the traditional medicines. As you investigate the claims made about herbs, extracts and mineral supplements for treating ADHD symptoms, try to ask yourself questions like the following:

Is the literature about this product believable? If you look for information on the Internet about herbal remedies for ADHD, you may find that a large percentage of the links and sites are providing marketing hype instead of unbiased, objective information.

Is there any independent confirmation about the product's effects? Find out who ran the tests that support the claims about the herbal treatment. Is there any credible research done on it, or is it just a commercial for the product?

Is there anyone using this for their own ADHD? If the article says "thousands of people nationwide are using this," then you need to know how many of those thousands are actually using it for their ADHD. How effective has it been for those people?

Are there any potential side effects? You need to know if there are any side effects for taking a particular herb. Some herbs have diuretic or laxative qualities. Some herbs should not be used in conjunction with other medications. Therefore, you need to consult a pharmacist or licensed medical practitioner to get the facts.

What you decide to use as part of your ADHD management is a personal decision. What you choose to use should not be based on any one factor, but on careful investigation of all factors, such as lifestyle, cost, effectiveness, and what you are comfortable with. You need to be an informed health care consumer.

In the interest of providing you with some basic information to get you started, we list below some of the more commonly-cited herbal alternatives to traditional medicines for treating ADHD. Our review here is not meant to be an endorsement of these products, and there is much written about these herbs and extracts (both pro and con) that you should review so you can decide if these might be right for you.

Pycnogenol (pronounced pick-nah-geh-nol) is a patented extract from the bark of the French Maritime Pine Tree. Pycnogenol is not a drug, it is a water soluble nutrient like Vitamin C. As an antioxidant supplement, Pycnogenol is actually 20 times more powerful than Vitamin C, and 50 times more powerful than Vitamin E. Pycnogenol is now available in the U.S. without a prescription. Results reported by Pycnogenol users typically include: a generalized calming effect, increased mental alertness, reduced impulsive behavior, decreased aggressiveness, more in control of one's thoughts, marked improvement in the ability to remain still, less noisiness and disruptive behavior.

Grape Seed Extract (an antioxidant). Considered a cheaper alternative to Pycnogenol, although there is debate both pro and con about its overall effectiveness. It is claimed that Grape Seed extract contains the identical proanthocyanidins as Pycnogenol, but in a slightly higher concentration (95 percent). You can find Grape Seed Extract in most health food and vitamin stores. Users of Grape Seed Extract claim to achieve better control over impulsiveness and hyperactivity, increased concentration, and an overall calming effect.

St. John's Wort (Hypericum perforatum) standardized for 0.3 percent hypericin. St. John's Wort has been getting more mention in the mainstream press lately as the safer herbal alternative to Prozac. Users claim that it works as a soothing mood stabilizer for people with ADHD, helping with depression and irritability. St. John's Wort can be found in most health food stores, and even in many drug stores and supermarkets.

Kava (Piper methysticum). This herb is used for its soothing, calming effect. Buy only a Kava product that is standardized to contain 25 percent kavalactones, as this is considered to be the most effective concentration.

Lemon Balm (melissa officinalis). This herb helps reduce nervous excitability. Look for Lemon Balm products that are standardized to contain 5 percent rosmarinic acid, which is the main beneficial ingredient.

Stramonium (thorn apple). This is used for decreasing anxiety and anger.

Hyoscyamus (henbane) is used to reduce silliness, loud speech, jealousy and aggressive behavior.

Veratrum Album (white hellebore). Users claim that they achieve greater concentration and are less argumentative when they take veratrum album.

Other herbs that are purportedly used to treat ADHD symptoms that you might want to learn more about are:

- Valerian root extract (mixed in any juice of your choice).
- Chamomile
- Passion flower
- Ginkgo
- Catnip
- Damiana
- Gotu Kola

More clinical studies need to be done to further measure the effectiveness of such herbal treatments, specifically for ADHD. If you are interested in taking advantage of these and other herbal treatments for your ADHD child, first go to your local library and/or search the Internet to gather as much information as you can. While these herbs can often be purchased in a store near you without a prescription, nevertheless we highly recommend that you consult a licensed medical professional to discuss recommended dosages and ask questions to help you set up a carefully monitored program for your ADHD child.

Nutrition and ADHD Behavior

Although not common, some children's ADHD symptoms may be affected by their diet. In 1975 a pediatrician-allergist named Benjamin Feingold wrote a book titled, *Why Your Child is Hyperactive*. In the book, he proposed that synthetic flavors and food coloring were related to hyperactivity. In the following years, subsequent research into a dietary relationship with ADHD behavior showed that only a small percentage of ADHD children (1 or 2 percent) showed improvement under a controlled dietary program.

Proponents of dietary modification claim that 50 percent of children with learning or attention problems can be cured by their methods, with another 25 percent showing considerable improvement. Critics of this approach point to the lack of convincing scientific data. Obviously, emotions run high on both sides of the diet debate.

Some parents report that their ADHD child seems to become more hyperactive after eating foods with a lot of sugar. Studies conducted so far indicate that sugar does *not* have a great effect on ADHD behavior. It may be possible, however, that refined sugars do increase the hyperactivity of some ADHD children if the blood sugar level is high enough. When a child's blood carbohydrate level is high (such as after eating a high carbohydrate breakfast), and the child is then given some candy or other high-sugar food, the child's activity level may go up.

Artificial sweeteners like aspartame (used in Equal® and NutraSweet®) have also been suspected of making ADHD children more aggressive or non-compliant when given in large amounts. However, there is no evidence that consumption of artificial sweeteners leads to adverse behaviors.

Some proponents of dietary modification say that food allergies are among the most common causes of learning and behavioral problems in children. Dr. Doris Rapp, a pediatrician and allergist in Buffalo, New York, contends that the number of children and adults who suffer from allergies or sensitivities to foods and environmental substances may exceed three-quarters of the U.S. population. Dr. Rapp asserts that offending substances are not only in our food, but in our drinking water, medicines and cosmetics, the clothes we wear, the houses we live in, and even in the air we breathe. Some ADHD children have been found to have allergies to certain foods. Some common dietary allergens are wheat, corn, rice, oat, peas, soy, peanuts, milk, artificial colors, pure baker's chocolate, eggs, cane sugar, beef, pork, tomato, potato, orange, lettuce, broccoli, green beans, coffee, and cheese.

While dietary causes for some aspects of ADHD behavior are not common, they may be explored together with your physician. If you suspect any allergic or dietary cause for your child's behavior, let your physician know about it, so proper tests can be done to determine if a special dietary program should be developed for your ADHD child.

Controversial Treatments

CHADD (Children and Adults with Attention Deficit/Hyperactivity Disorders) is a national association that provides support and information about ADHD. The organization also monitors developments in treating ADHD, and issues official statements for the reference and guidance of parents and others working with ADHD children and adults. This section of the book summarizes positions that CHADD has taken on several controversial treatments for ADHD.

Many treatments have been scientifically proven to be effective for children with ADHD. These include behavior management, parent training and the use of medications. However, seemingly impressive claims have been made about treatments that are unproven or yet to be evaluated in accord with scientific standards. Parents should be wary of investing time,

money and their child's health and well-being in unproven, questionable treatments. Parents are cautioned to be suspicious of:

- overstated and exaggerated claims;
- treatments that claim to treat a wide variety of ailments;
- testimonials from people claiming to have been helped by a treatment, since enthusiasm is no substitute for scientific evidence; and
- any claim that a treatment is being suppressed or unfairly attacked by the "medical establishment."

EEG biofeedback for treatment of children with ADHD has been controversial and remains as yet an unproven treatment. Proponents of biofeedback believe that children with ADHD can be trained to increase the type of brain-wave activity associated with sustained attention. Up to 20 electrodes are attached to the child's head. Levels of electrical activity in various parts of the brain are measured and entered into a computer. The computer provides a signal, such as a light or tone. This "feedback" is supposed to teach the child to increase certain kinds of brain-wave activity and decrease other types. Training usually involves 40-80 sessions, each lasting 40 minutes or more. This "treatment" costs $3,000 to $6,000.

CHADD contends that the studies which suggest impressive results for EEG biofeedback are seriously flawed. Sample sizes were small and appropriate control groups were not used to determine if any results are due to maturation or an "expectancy" effect. Parents considering the use of biofeedback should proceed with caution.

Another controversial and unproven theory maintains that ADHD is caused by problems in the inner ear system. Advocates of this theory recommend an array of medications including anti-motion sickness medications and several vitamin-like substances. A success rate of more than 90% has been claimed for this treatment.

However, this is anecdotal and has not been published in professional journals. No scientific support from well-controlled investigations has been offered. This theory is completely inconsistent with current knowledge of ADHD.

Some have even linked ADHD to yeast. Candida albicans is a type of yeast that lives in the human body. At times candida can overgrow, causing, for example, a vaginal yeast infection known as Candidiasis. Those who support an ADHD-candida link believe that toxins produced by yeast overgrowth weaken the immune system. The body then becomes susceptible to ADHD and other disorders. Treatment consists of antifungal medication and a low-sugar diet, as sugar is believed to stimulate yeast growth. There is no evidence to support this theory and it is not consistent with current knowledge of ADHD.

Another controversial theory suggests that ADHD is caused by a genetic abnormality resulting in increased requirements for vitamins and minerals. A treatment regimen—debunked 20 years ago—involves extremely high doses of vitamins.

Others have suggested that ADHD is caused by the misalignment of two bones in the skull and promote the use of bodily manipulations to restore these bones to their proper position.

Parents can indeed become desperate for a "silver bullet" treatment, and in their desperation may be vulnerable to exaggerated or misleading claims. In this book, we want to inform parents about appropriate as well as controversial treatments. We urge parents to only provide their children treatments that have been scientifically proven to be safe and effective.

---

*Medication information provided in part by Hugh W. Ridlehuber, M.D., F.A.B.P., Child and Adult Psychiatrist, Belmont, California, and Kim Conner-Kuhn Pharm. D., Charge Pharmacist at Mills Peninsula Health Services, Mills Peninsula Hospital, Burlingame, California.

CHAPTER 9

The Parent/Teacher Survival Guide

Your Right to Sanity

Up to this point in the book, we have discussed the many things that can be done to help your child manage his or her behavior. Now it is fitting that we dedicate a chapter to you—the parents and teachers—to give you some advice and guidance on how to cope with your child's behavior without losing your sanity in the process. We have summarized a few of the more successful and widely used strategies for managing behavior of children with ADHD. We conclude the chapter with practical advice on looking after yourself to help you survive the daily challenges of living and working with your child.

10 Guiding Principles

Dr. Russell A. Barkley developed 10 general principles for parents and teachers to use when dealing with a child with ADHD. He recommends that you tape a copy of the 10 Guiding Principles to your mirror or wall, so you can be reminded each day. These 10 principles are as follows:

1. **Give immediate feedback and consequences.**
   Children with ADHD live in the moment. You must react at that moment.

Don't wait several minutes or hours later to praise or correct your child.

2. **Give more frequent feedback.**
   Because of their shorter attention spans and tendency to forget past events, ADHD children need feedback more frequently than other kids. Try to encourage or instruct the child at regular intervals.

3. **Use larger, more powerful consequences.**
   Words alone are usually not enough to motivate a child with ADHD. Use hugs, special snacks or treats, tokens or points, or (if appropriate) material rewards to reinforce desired behavior.

4. **Use incentives before punishment.**
   If punishment is used by itself or without consistent positive feedback, it is not very effective at changing behavior. Remember the rule–positives before negatives. Replace undesirable behaviors with positive ones. Emphasize points and rewards. Do not punish for every single thing your child does wrong. Instead, punish consistently but selectively for certain misbehaviors.

5. Strive for consistency.

Use the same strategies for dealing with your child's behavior every time. Make sure both parents and teachers are using the same techniques. Respond the same way at home, at school or in public places.

6. Act, don't yak!

Stop lecturing your child. Use consequences instead. Consequences speak louder and clearer to an ADHD child than talking ever does. If your child is misbehaving, simply count out loud from one to three. If the child doesn't stop, he goes for a time-out. No stalling for time, nor any delays. Just act.

7. Plan ahead for problem situations.

You know when and where your child tends to misbehave. Decide what you will do in those situations, and let your child know about your plan. Follow these steps before entering a potential problem situation:

1. Stop and review two or three simple rules with your child.
2. Explain the reward you'll give for good behavior.
3. Explain what punishment will be used for misbehavior.
4. Follow your plan as you enter the situation. Give immediate positive feedback for good behavior, or swift punishment for misbehavior.

8. Keep a disability perspective.

Remember that your child is behaviorally disabled. Your child cannot help acting that way! Keep your cool in upsetting situations by maintaining a psychological distance from your child's problems. If you remind yourself each day that your child cannot control his behavior, you can react more reasonably, fairly and rationally.

9. Don't personalize your child's problems or disorder.

Don't think that you are a bad parent when a situation goes wrong. Do not make your child feel guilty or inadequate for behavior he cannot control. Don't try to win arguments with your child. Stay calm, and do not let your personal dignity or self-worth be determined by your child's behavior.

10. Practice forgiveness.

Every day, let go of your anger, bitterness, resentment, disappointment or other negative feelings caused by your child's behavior. You must hold your child accountable for misbehavior, but do not feel bitter toward your child. Also, forgive others who misunderstood your child's behavior and criticized you as a parent. And forgive yourself for any mistakes you made that day managing your child's behavior.

In addition to the above, Peter Jaska, Ph.D., points out to parents and teachers that they should maintain a sense of humor and a lot of patience. Stay focused on the goals for your child, yourself, and your family. Parents and teachers must also expect variability of performance. ADHD children have good days and bad days, and thus will not always perform or respond in the same way each time. Finally, be an informed consumer; educate yourself about ADHD.

Classroom Techniques for the Young Child with ADHD

Teachers face unique challenges in helping children with ADHD be successful in school. Below is a list of accommodations that teachers may employ in the classroom to assist young ADHD children. Generally, these accommodations are easy to implement and very effective.

Memory and Attention
- Seat the ADHD child close to the teacher.
- Keep the child away from distractions (noisy classmates, windows, etc.)
- Secure attention before giving directions.
- Maintain eye contact throughout presentations.
- Keep oral instructions brief. Repeat, repeat, repeat.
- Check to ensure understanding. Have the child repeat back your directions.
- Make projects interesting: use visual aids.
- Match projects to the child's interests and skills.
- Use flash cards, rhymes, cues to enhance memory.

Impulse Control
- Remind the child to keep his hands to himself (i.e., fold arms, keep hands in pockets).
- Coach the child to stop and think before he acts.
- Redirect the child to another activity if he misbehaves.
- Provide outlets to help the child let off steam.
- Coach the child to be self-observant of his or her own behavior.

- Watch out for overstimulation. Use guidelines to prevent the child from losing control.
- Prior to quiet activities, encourage physical exercise

Structure
- Make your expectations clear–post rules, repeat directions.
- Set limits and stick to them.
- Impose moderate but consistent discipline.
- State consequences clearly for unacceptable behavior.
- Keep the child busy with projects; limit unstructured free play time.
- Prepare for unstructured time.
- Establish a daily routine, with predictable transitions between activities.
- Use a timer to mark the end of activities.

Productivity
- Break up large tasks into small steps.
- Use imaginative play to keep the child on task.
- Ask the child what will help him or her to complete tasks.
- Monitor and measure progress often: use a chart or point system.

Self-Esteem
- Reward any progress, no matter how small.
- Be on the lookout to catch the child doing good.
- Praise, pat on the back, approve, encourage.
- Encourage performance in the child's area of strength.
- Avoid humiliation. Don't ask the child to do difficult tasks in front of others.
- Give responsibilities and leadership roles to the child to boost his confidence.

- Use a simple behavioral report card for the child to bring home each day.

Social Relationships

- Provide feedback about behavior in social situations with other children.
- Role play proper social behavior with the child.
- Encourage the child to use their words express their emotions with others.
- Help the child identify and understand nonverbal cues.
- Separate the ADHD child from other children with emotional/behavioral problems.

Self-Esteem for Parents

As the parent of a child with ADHD, ask yourself honestly if you often find yourself distorting or overemphasizing the negative things that the child does, or forget the positive things. As human beings, we tend to emphasize faults. Parents, in particular, struggle with guilty feelings because repeated irritations foster a dislike of their ADHD child. Some parents even blame themselves as the cause of the ADHD child's problems. You probably forget many positive things your ADHD child does each day, the little things that often go unnoticed. Take time to notice them. Also, take time to give yourself due credit for everything you do to keep things going. You need to build your self-esteem as much as your child needs to build hers.

Coping with ADHD

Take time to cope with the stress your child's ADHD is causing you. Don't let the stress of the moment or your adrenaline force you to act rashly or impulsively toward your child. Give yourself a time-out by walking away from the situation and cooling off in your bedroom. You can learn deep breathing or muscle-relaxing techniques to relax yourself.

Another important thing to remember is not to let yourself become bogged down in the little details, or let things get blown out of proportion. Keep in your mind the vision of how you want things resolved as you deal with each situation.

You can find a hobby or activity that interests you. Perhaps membership in a club would give you a welcome diversion from your daily troubles. You could join a support group of ADHD parents. You could get involved in your local church, mosque, synagogue, or community organization.

Renew friendships. Get in touch with friends, and enjoy their company. They can provide a listening ear and a shoulder to lean on if you need it.

You can work out a tag-team parenting effort with your spouse to share the burden of dealing with your child. You can also work out a cooperative arrangement with other parents to form play groups or babysitting circles. This will give you time to pursue your other interests and have a little time off.

Take time to stop and smell the roses. There could be wonderful things happening around you, but you could be too busy to notice. Take time to stop and appreciate a sunset or sunrise, the color of tree leaves, watch some ants working, or admire the colors of flowers. You could take a short walk around the block and just enjoy some fresh air.

Avoid habits that work against you and your health. If you smoke, or drink alcohol or caffeine beverages, evaluate your habits. Nicotine and caffeine are stimulants that adversely affect your heart, blood pressure, breathing rate, muscle tension, and add more stress to your body than you want. Alcohol causes fatigue, irritability, and withdrawal. In short, smoking and drinking take a lot out of you, so why add to your stress?

Events in life don't stress us out, it is how we react to those events that stresses us. To manage stress more effectively, you must control your thoughts. You must cultivate an optimistic attitude. A theologian once said: "Attitude determines altitude." If you think negative, critical thoughts, you're going to be crabby and miserable. On the other hand, if you think positive, constructive thoughts, you can diminish negative emotions that lead to stress.

Remember that everyone makes mistakes. The key is to learn from the mistakes and not do them again. Think about something that happened, the solution you took, and why it didn't work. What would you do differently next time? Try to take time to evaluate each day, and the mistakes you made, and plan what you'll do next time.

Remember to take good care of yourself. Manage your time so that you can set aside time for yourself. Eat right, and exercise. If you can arrange for your spouse, a relative or a baby-sitter to watch your child for you, then you can recharge your emotional batteries by taking a weekend vacation, or a few hours of free time away from your child.

The mother typically bears the larger share of the burden of looking after the ADHD child, and this subjects her to a higher level of frustration. The child often becomes her all-consuming focus, and the mother usually spends less time with her spouse and other children. It is not uncommon for mothers to become highly depressed after years and years of stress, and some even turn to substance abuse. They can also become critical of their own parenting skills, and they may even blame themselves for their predicament. Family members need to ease the mother's burden by taking on some of the responsibilities of caring for the child.

Marriages are often put into jeopardy because of the constant stress, struggle and daily unpredictability of dealing with an ADHD child. Intimacy between spouses is often the first thing to suffer because of resentment, financial concerns, lack of time, exhaustion, child care demands, feelings of disappointment,

etc. All of this puts a horrendous strain on the marriage relationship. Often spouses do not realize that the friction in their relationship is being caused by the ADHD child's behavior, not their own.

If the mother had an unpleasant experience with the ADHD child in the morning, the frustration or anger from the incident may fester all day long, only to manifest itself later with the spouse in an unrelated matter.

It is important to seek professional help when feelings of depression, inadequacy and problems in your relationship start to overwhelm you. In addition, you and your spouse can take positive steps on your own, such as :

- Keep talking with your spouse about your feelings, and how each day went.
- Be sure to support, not blame, each other.
- Go on a date with your spouse each week.
- Do something nice for each other, each day.
- Always try to keep realistic expectations of each other. Don't expect perfection from each other or your child.

CHAPTER 10

Lives Changed:
Putting this Book's Principles into Practice

Getting the Hang of It

As an approach to managing ADHD, redirection is easy but it isn't applied as much as it should be. Although it only takes a few hours to read this book to get a grasp of practical knowledge and to learn the techniques to deal with ADHD behavior, like parenting it could take years, or perhaps a lifetime, to really master it all.

ADHD, it turns out, does not exhibit any neat, predictable characteristics. ADHD is as varied as the multitude of children it affects. Many decisions that parents and teachers of young children with ADHD have to make are often reached in the face of insufficient information about the nature of ADHD, and a lack of knowledge of techniques and strategies to deal with it. We hope that this guidebook helps to remedy that situation.

Everything we have introduced in this guidebook will give parents and teachers of ADHD youngsters the practical know-how, tools and intervention techniques that they need to effectively manage ADHD behavior in a variety of situations. Used in conjunction with the *Buzz & Pixie Activity Coloring Book*, this guidebook promises to be a valuable reference to help you handle most of the challenges that you are likely to encounter.

As we bring this guidebook to a conclusion, you are probably wondering how the lives of yourself and your ADHD child will change as you put the principles of this book into practice. ADHD is such a dynamic, multi-varied disorder that it would be impossible to predict exactly how the techniques in this guidebook will impact any given situation. However, you are certain to see positive changes from your consistent use of redirection and by implementing a comprehensive treatment approach.

To give you an idea of how all of this can benefit you, let us revisit the three families that we introduced at the beginning of this guidebook, and see the end result of the concepts, advice, and techniques we have advocated.

Joey & Family
Fortified and Flourishing

Joey's parents, Alan and Lisa, have learned to channel Joey's early morning energy into constructive activity to allow them a little more precious sleep each morning. Joey still wakes up early, but Joey's parents have put the principle of redirection to work to keep him from pouncing on them in bed. They lay out some crayons and plenty of paper and coloring books on the dining room table for Joey to work on until they wake up. When Alan and Lisa wake up, Joey shows off his handiwork for the morning. Joey glows with pride as his parents warmly praise his artwork, and they put the pictures in a special scrapbook and talk about them before having breakfast.

Learning that ADHD children respond to well-structured schedules, Joey's parents have instituted a morning schedule for him which helps make the mornings less stressful for everyone. They have make a colorful chart of Joey's morning schedule, and review it with Joey frequently so he knows the routine. Joey now enjoys the security of knowing that he will get the attention of his parents if he leaves them alone to sleep a little longer while he works on his drawings, and he knows that he must get dressed for school before he has breakfast. His clothes are laid out the night before, thus avoiding any last minute hassles over getting dressed. With everything in its proper place and time, mornings at Joey's house have become far more pleasant and manageable than ever before.

Occasionally, Joey wakes up a little too giddy or wiggly, and may get into trouble. Alan and Lisa have learned to watch for the warning signals that precede any misbehavior and intervene by redirecting Joey to another activity.

Most of the time this works quite well, but when Joey does not respond or cooperate, Alan and Lisa have employed the 1-2-3 Rule. They simply say, "Joey, that's 1!" when they see him start to escalate out of control. If Joey doesn't stop, they say, "Joey, that's 2!."

Alan and Lisa learned that they should not lecture Joey, but rather just count out the warnings. When Joey continues to misbehave after two warnings, they simply say, "Joey, that's three. Take five minutes for time-out!" They escort Joey to his room or a designated time-out corner. They may be sending Joey's imaginary friend, Sparky, along with him to commiserate. This unemotional, no-nonsense 1-2-3 approach has helped diffuse any power struggle between Joey and his parents, because it makes Joey accountable to the rules for his actions. In an effort to help Joey reflect more meaningfully on his actions, his parents ask Joey to talk about his misbehavior with Sparky during his time-out, and draw a picture depicting the incident.

To Alan and Lisa's surprise, they have noticed that their positive parenting efforts and spending more quality time with Joey have helped him alleviate his morbid depression, and they see that his pictures have stopped being morose, dark and gloomy. Joey now proudly shows off colorful, exuberant pictures of himself and other characters in various creative settings. Joey also seems less on edge nowadays, and is more comfortable in his relationship with his parents.

Over time, Alan has learned to not take Joey's misbehavior personally, and has redirected his thinking by taking a disability perspective regarding his son's ADHD. Alan now knows that Joey cannot help it sometimes, and this perspective helps him deal with Joey in a more loving, understanding and non-judgmental way. Alan has also learned to communicate with his wife more often about his feelings in parenting Joey, and together they plan strategies to motivate Joey toward achieving goals.

Joey's teacher at school, Ms. Reynoso, has also seen a positive change in Joey's behavior in class. Joey seems to be more connected with his classmates, and cooperates in play more often. He still has times when he grows listless and aimless, and strays off-task in certain activities.

However, Ms. Reynoso has learned to watch for the warning signs that precede Joey's misbehavior, and is usually able to intervene or redirect him before he loses control.

When Joey loses control, Ms. Reynoso tries to alternate time-outs with redirection in order to avoid a continuous string of punishments and harm Joey's self-esteem. Ms. Reynoso talks frequently with Joey's parents to make sure that she is aware of their goals for Joey, and together they have devised a simple progress chart using smiley faces to indicate how Joey is doing each day at school. This helps provide feedback and helps Joey measure his own progress.

Ricky & Family
Medication and Redirection

Remember Joyce, the single mother, and little Ricky, her very busy little boy? They've made much progress since the last time we saw them.

Joyce learned that Ricky likes to keep his hands busy, so she decided to set up several activity spots around the dining room table, one spot with Legos®, another with Playdough®, another with Tinker Toys®, and so on. Joyce reviews the rules with Ricky for each activity spot.

When Joey wakes up, he plays at each spot contentedly for half an hour while Joyce gets breakfast ready. Joyce has observed Ricky and saw that he had a great creative capacity, in addition to a need to keep his hands busy. So, Joyce has looked for toys which are simple yet allow for some assembly, such as jigsaw puzzles, Legos®, Lincoln Logs®, and others.

Joyce has come to accept the dimensions of Ricky's ADHD, and sought counseling for herself and assessment for Ricky. After careful assessment, it was determined that Ricky's hyperactivity and his depression, were getting in the way of his learning, and hindering Joyce's parenting efforts.

Ricky was put on small dosages of medications under careful supervision, and within a few days Joyce has noticed that Ricky is now more affectionate, responsive socially, can concentrate better, and has fewer emotional outbursts. It was as if the "real" Ricky had surfaced, after being in hiding all his life. Ricky was now a sweet, caring, sensitive child who was very creative and bright. Joyce keeps care-

ful record of Ricky's behavior while on medication, and reports regularly to his doctor.

At school, Joyce has worked closely with Ricky's teacher to ensure that both she and the teacher operate from the same disciplinary procedures for home and at school. The teacher had the foresight to enlist Ricky as her "little helper" in class, and he earns tokens as points which he trades in for colorful stickers at the end of the class day. Both Joyce and Ricky's teacher coach Ricky on how to express his feelings in words, and he has shown good progress.

Since Ricky's ability to concentrate has dramatically improved due to the medication, Joyce and Ricky's teacher are now able to try out various techniques to help him learn better than he has in the past.

Joyce works with Ricky at home by making a simple "desired behaviors" chart, with three simple rules on it: Sit still at the table; No running inside the house; No loud voices inside the house. Joyce places stickers on the chart when Ricky achieves mastery of the rules.

As the day winds down, Joyce has found redemption in routines. She has established a nightly bedtime routine for Ricky: take a warm bath; then storytime with Hypie the Hummingbird, a glass of warm milk, and then a tuck-in song. The tuck-in song has quickly become Ricky's favorite ritual: Joyce will hold Ricky upside-down at the ankles, and gently swing him side-to-side like a pendulum as she sings the nursery rhyme, *Hickory Dickory Dock.* Ricky enjoys the tummy tickle as "the mouse runs up and down the clock." Then Joyce gently swings Ricky into his bed for a quiet tuck-in. Such a bedtime routine has helped Joyce and Ricky bond closer over the months.

Exhausted but pleased, Joyce flops into bed, and reflects on her day. She and Ricky have made great progress. Once she overcame her initial reluctance about medication and counseling, she was able to implement a unified, integrated treatment program with the cooperation of Ricky's teacher and mental health professionals. She could feel Ricky responding favorably and she was feeling more rewarded for her parenting efforts. Parenting Ricky was still full of challenges, but Joyce now feels that she and Ricky are progressing together, and growing closer in the process.

Suzy and Family
Focused and Feeling Better

Little Suzy now goes to a special play group composed of other ADHD children, where trained professionals help each child learn to socialize and interact. Suzy's parents, George and Lindsay, were told about the play group by the therapist, and they eagerly signed Suzy up for enrollment. Instead of spacing-out, as was her usual custom, Suzy has now learned to stay on-task, and is more aware of the activities of other children around her in the play group.

Suzy's presence in the play group marked a major milestone for George and Lindsay. First, George and Lindsay had to come to terms that there was something wrong with Suzy, and seek help. To come to terms with their denial, they sought the counsel of a psychologist, who advised them to cut back on some of the extracurricular activities they were putting Suzy through and simply spend more quality time with her.

The psychologist also recommended that they help Suzy develop an imaginary friend and use that friend in their playtime with Suzy. Lindsay and George would often have conversations with Suzy's pretend friend, "Tiffany," and use Tiffany to help Suzy learn how to obey household rules or think of playtime ideas. Suzy draws pictures of Tiffany and hangs them on her bedroom walls, and George and Lindsay have even bought a special toothbrush, cup, pillow and other accessories just for Tiffany to use. All of this has helped Suzy to become more extroverted, and less spacey.

While George and Lindsay have cut-down on the extracurricular activities, one activity that they kept was Suzy's participation on the soccer team. George would notice that Suzy would still "space-out" on the field at times, so he and Suzy devised a special code word which he could yell out to help her snap out of it without drawing any embarrassing attention to herself. When George would notice his daughter start to trail off, distracted, he would yell out "Snicklefritz!" Suzy would know that this meant she had to keep her eye on the ball, and she would re-enter the action of the game, newly refocused.

After tucking-in little Suzy each night, George and Lindsay would spend a few minutes together reviewing the events of the day and plan out their goals and strategies for tomorrow. Coming to terms with their daughter's ADHD has helped them to unite their talents in planning out a course for success for little Suzy.

George and Lindsay have also started making time for each other nowadays: they call Aunt Mildred to arrange babysitting for Suzy so they can enjoy a romantic weekend getaway!

Now It Is Up To You

As you embark on your own program for your ADHD child's improvement, we want to assure you that there are many positive aspects to raising an ADHD child. With your loving participation and guidance, you will have the deep satisfaction of watching your ADHD child grow to lead a successful life.

Consider how fortunate your child is, that you are willing to put in the time and effort to follow the guidelines in this book. Remember, you will make progress! Don't let any setbacks along the way overshadow your successes.

Most importantly, the quality of time with your child, your resourcefulness, persistence, dedication and acceptance are valuable in helping your ADHD youngster grow in self-esteem, and set the foundation for lifelong success.

We have worked hard to make *ADHD and the Young Child* as informative and useful as possible. When you put the principles of this book into practice and frequently review the cartoon scenarios, you can spend productive time shaping the behavior of your ADHD child.

We are vitally interested in learning of our readers' achievements as they put the principles of this guidebook into practice in their lives. We encourage parents and teachers of young ADHD children to write to us, in care of the publisher, to share their stories of success, or share any suggestions for future editions.

References

Chapter 2

Barkley, R. (1993). *Taking charge of ADHD: The complete, authoritative guide for parents.* New York. Guilford Press. Pgs. 17-19, 29, 55-76.

Dinkmeyer, D. Sr., MacKay, G., & Dinkmeyer, J. (1989). *Parenting young children.* Circle Pines, Minnesota.: American Guidance Service. Pgs. 129, 132-135, 140-147.

Gordon, S., & Asher, M. (1994). *Meeting the ADD challenge: A practical guide for teachers.* Champaign, Illinois: Research Press. Pgs. 18-20, 26, 32, 46.

Ingersoll, B., & Goldstein, S. (1993). *Attention deficit disorder and learning disabilities: Realities, myths and controversial treatments,* New York: Doubleday Mainstreet Books. Pgs. 27-28, 62-63.

Silver, L. (1993). *Dr. Larry Silver's advice to parents on attention-deficit hyperactivity disorder.* Washington, D.C.: American Psychiatric Press, Inc. Pgs. 44-51, 82-86, 88-89.

Taylor, J. (1994). *Helping your hyperactive/attention deficit child, 2nd edition.* Rocklin, Calif.: Prima Publishing.

Chapter 3

Dinkmeyer, D. Sr., MacKay, G., & Dinkmeyer, J. S. (1989). *Parenting young children.* Circle Pines, Minnesota.: American Guidance Service. Pgs. 47-55, 135-139, 142-143.

Barkley, R. (1993). *Taking charge of ADHD: The complete, authoritative guide for parents.* New York. Guilford Press.

Phelan, T. (1993). *All about attention deficit disorder.* Glen Ellyn, Illinois: Child Management, Inc. Pgs. 74-75, 78-79.

Taylor, J. (1994). *Helping your hyperactive/attention deficit child, 2nd edition,* Rocklin, Calif.: Prima Publishing.

Chapter 4

Barkley, R. (1993). *Taking charge of ADHD: The complete, authoritative guide for parents.* New York. Guilford Press. Pgs. 198-199.

Dinkmeyer, D. Sr., MacKay, G., & Dinkmeyer, J. (1989). *Parenting young children.* Circle Pines, Minnesota.: American Guidance Service. Pgs. 55-57, 68-71, 74-78.

Quinn, P., & Stern, J. (1993). *The putting on the brakes activity book for young people with ADHD.* New York: Magination Press. Pg. 25.

Chapter 5

Braswell, L., & Bloomquist, M.(1991). *Cognitive behavioral therapy with ADHD children: Child, family and school interventions.* New York: The Guilford Press. Pg. 149.

Dinkmeyer, D. Sr., MacKay, G., & Dinkmeyer, J. (1989). *Parenting young children.* Circle Pines, Minnesota.: American Guidance Service. Pgs. 105-116.

Gordon, S., & Asher, M. (1994). *Meeting the ADD challenge: A practical guide for teachers.* Champaign, Illinois: Research Press. Pgs. 21-22, 97-100, 105-111, 114-116.

Johnson, D. (1992). *I can't sit still: Educating and affirming inattentive and hyperactive children.* Santa Cruz, Calif.: ETR Associates. Pgs. 39-43.

Segal, M. *(1985). Your child at play: Two to three Yyarsógrowing up, language, and the imagination.* New York.: Newmarket Press. Pgs. 139-149.

Silver, L. (1993). *Dr. Larry Silver's advice to parents on attention-deficit hyperactivity disorder.* Washington, D.C.: American Psychiatric Press, Inc. Pgs. 155-167.

Chapter 7

Barkley, R. (1993). *Taking charge of ADHD: The complete, authoritative guide for parents.* New York. Guilford Press. Pgs. 103-105.

Gordon, S., & Asher, M. (1994). *Meeting the ADD challenge: A practical guide for teachers.* Champaign, Illinois: Research Press. Pgs. 74-75.

Phelan, T. (1993). *All about attention deficit disorder.* Glen Ellyn, Illinois: Child Management, Inc. Pgs. 52-60.

Sattler, J. (1988). *Assessment of children. Third edition.* San Diego, California: Jerome M. Sattler, Publisher, Pgs. 915-930.

Chapter 8

Barkley, R. (1993). *Taking charge of ADHD: The complete, authoritative guide for parents.* New York. Guilford Press. Pgs. 250-257.

CHADD (1995). Controversial Treatments for ADHD. Internet site: www.chadd.com.

Ingersoll, B., & Goldstein, S. (1993). *Attention deficit disorder and learning disabilities: Realities, myths and controversial treatments,* New York: Doubleday Mainstreet Books. Pgs. 149, 155-156.

Silver, L. (1993). *Dr. Larry Silver's advice to parents on attention-deficit hyperactivity disorder.* Washington, D.C.: American Psychiatric Press, Inc. Pgs. 145-149, 173-178, 199-203.

Taylor, J. (1994). *Helping your hyperactive/attention deficit child, 2nd edition,* Rocklin, Calif.: Prima Publishing. Pgs. 47-62, 63-95, and 97-100.

Chapter 9

Alexander-Roberts, C. (1994). *The ADHD parenting handbook.* Dallas, Texas: Taylor Publishing Company. Pgs. 182-186.

Barkley, R. (1993). *Taking charge of ADHD: The complete, authoritative guide for parents.* New York. Guilford Press. Pgs. Pgs. 130-136 and 139-145.

Emerson, S., & Baren, M. *What ADHD is-and isn't...and what to do.* (Patient Care, July 1996) Pgs. 26-51.

Hallowell, E., & Ratey, J. (1996). *Answers to distraction,* New York: Bantam Books. Pgs. 83-91.

Jaska, P. (1996). *Top 10 rules for parents and teachers of children with ADHD,* Online Psychological Services

Phelan, T. (1993). *All about attention deficit disorder.* Glen Ellyn, Illinois: Child Management, Inc. Pg. 76.

Quinn, P., & Stern, J. (1993.) *The "Putting on the Brakes" activity book for young people with ADHD.* New York: Magination Press. Pg. 21.

Index

APPENDIX A

ADHD
Support Services for Parents

Parent Organizations

CHADD
Children with Attention Deficit/Hyperactivity
Disorder
National Headquarters
8181 Professional Place
Landover, MD 20785
(800) 233-4050
www.chadd.org

CHADD is a national alliance of parent organizations that provides information and support to parents of children with ADHD.

ADDA
National Attention Deficit Disorder
Association
P.O. Box 1303
Northbrook, Illinois 60065-1303

ADDA is a national alliance of ADHD support groups that provides referrals and information to parents and parent support groups.

LDA
Learning Disabilities Association of America
4156 Library Road
Pittsburgh, Pennsylvania, 15234
(412) 341-1515

LDA is a national organization with state, county, and local chapters for parents of children and adolescents with learning disabilities and adults with learning disabilities. Provides information on the disorder and on available services.

Professional Organizations

American Academy of Child and Adolescent
Psychiatry
3615 Wisconsin Ave., N.W.
Washington, D.C., 20016
(202) 966-7300

American Academy of Pediatrics
P.O. Box 927
141 Northwest Point Blvd.
Elk Grove Village, Illinois, 60009
(708) 981-7935

American Psychiatric Association
1400 K Street, N.W.
Washington, D.C., 20002
(800) 368-5777
(202) 336-5500

American Psychological Association
750 1st Street, N.E.
Washington, D.C. 20002-4242
(202) 336-5500

Attention Deficit Information Network
(Ad-IN)
475 Hillside Ave.,
Needham, MA, 02194
(617) 455-9895

Council for Exceptional Children
1920 Association Drive
Reston, Virginia, 22091
(703) 620-3660

Feingold Association of the U.S.
Box 6550
Alexandria, Virginia, 22306
(703) 768-FAUS

ADD WareHouse
300 NW 70th Ave., Suite 102
Plantation, Florida, 33317
(800) 233-9273 • (954) 792-8100
www.addwarehouse.com

Tourette's Syndrome Association
42-40 Bell Blvd.
Bayside, New York, 11361
(800) 237-0717

Parents' Educational Resource Center (PERC)
1660 South Amphlett Blvd., Suite 200
San Mateo, California, 94402-2508
(650)655-2410
(650) 655-2411 Fax

Other Organizations

Orton Dyslexia Society
724 York Road
Baltimore, Maryland, 21204
(301) 296-0232

National Center for Learning Disabilities
99 Park Avenue
New York, N.Y., 10016
(212) 687-7211

Self Help Clearing House
St. Claire's Riverside Medical Center
Pocono Road, Denville, New Jersey, 07834
(201) 625-9565

APPENDIX B

Suggested Readings & Videos

About ADHD for Parents and Teachers

Adamec, C. (2000). *Moms with ADD: A self help manual.* Dallas, Texas: Taylor Trade Publishing.

Armstrong, T. (1995). *The myth of the A.D.D. child: 50 ways to improve your child's behavior and attention span without drugs, labels, or coercion.* New York: Dutton Books.

Asher M., & Schleser R. (1988). *Self-instructional manual for teachers and other professionals working with attention-deficit hyperactivity disorder children.* (unpublished manuscript). Chicago, Illinois: Illinois Institute of Technology.

Alexander-Roberts, C. (1994). *The ADHD parenting handbook: Practical advice for parents from parents.* Dallas: Taylor Publishing Company.

Bain, L. (1991). *A parent's guide to attention deficit disorders.* New York: Delta/Dell Books.

Barkley, R. (2000). *Taking charge of ADHD (revised edition): The complete, authoritative guide for parents.* New York: The Guilford Press.

Barkley, R. (1992). *ADHD: What can we do?* New York: The Guilford Press. (Videotape Program)

Barkley, R. (1992). *ADHD: What do we know?* New York: The Guilford Press. (Videotape Program)

Barkley, R. (1990). *Attention deficit hyperactivity disorder: A handbook for diagnosis and treatment.* New York: The Guilford Press.

Braswell, L., & Bloomquist, M. (1991). *Cognitive-behavior therapy with ADHD children: Child, family and school interventions.* New York: The Guilford Press.

Campbell, S. (1990). *Behavioral problems in preschool children.* New York: The Guilford Press.

Fowler, M. (1990). *Maybe you know my kid: A parent's guide to identifying, understanding, and helping your child with ADHD.* New York: Birch Lane Press.

Fowler, M. (1992). *The CHADD educator's manual.* Plantation, Florida: CASET Associates.

Goldstein, S. (1992). *Hyperactivity: Why won't my child pay attention?* Salt Lake City, Utah: Neurology, Learning and Behavior Center.

Goldstein, S., & Goldstein, M. (1991). *It's just attention disorder: A video guide for kids.* Salt Lake City, Utah: Neurology, Learning and Behavior Center.

Goldstein, S., & Goldstein, M. (1989). *Why won't my child pay attention?* Salt Lake City, Utah: Neurology, Learning and Behavior Center.

Gordon, S., & Asher, M. (1994). *Meeting the ADD challenge: A practical guide for teachers.* Champaign, Illinois: Research Press.

Hallowell, E., & Ratey, J. (1994). *Driven to distraction.* New York: Simon & Schuster.

Heininger, J., & Weiss, S.K. (2001). *From Chaos to Calm: Effective Parenting of Challenging*

Children with ADHD and Other Behavioral Problems. New York: Perigree Books.

Johnson, D. (1992). *I can't sit still: Educating and affirming inattentive and hyperactive children.* Santa Cruz, California: ETR Associates.

Paine, S., Radicchi, J., Rosellini, L., Deutchman, L., & Darch, C. (1983). *Structuring your classroom for academic success.* Champaign, Illinois: Research Press.

Parker, H. (2005). *The ADHD workbook for parents.* Plantation, Florida: Specialty Press, Inc.

Parker H. (2005). *The ADHD handbook for schools.* Plantation, Florida: Specialty Press, Inc.

Parker, H. (2000). *Problem solver guide for students with ADHD.* Plantation, Florida: Specialty Press, Inc.

Phelan, T. (1993). *All about attention deficit disorder.* Illinois: Child Management Inc.

Phelan, T. (2003). *1-2-3 Magic: Effective discipline for children 2-12 (3rd Edition).* Glen Ellyn, Illinois: ParentMagic, Inc.

Phelan, T. (1990). *Attention deficit hyperactivity disorder* (Videotape Program). Illinois: Child Management Press.

Rief, S. F. (2005). *How to reach and teach children with ADD/ADHD. (2nd Edition).* New York: Jossey Bass.

Silver, L. (1993). *Dr. Larry Silver's advice to parents on attention-deficit hyperactivity disorder.* Washington D.C.: American Psychiatric Press, Inc.

Taylor, J. (1994). *Helping your hyperactive/attention deficit child.* Rocklin, California: Prima Publishing.

Woodrich, D. (1994). *Attention deficit hyperactivity disorder: What every parent wants to know.* Baltimore, MD. Paul H. Brookes Publishing Co.

Zentall, S. (1992). *Identification, assessment and management of ADHD youth in educational contexts.* Paper presented at the fourth annual conference on Attention Deficit Disorder. Chicago, Illinois: CH.A.D.D.

About ADHD for Children

Corman, C., & Trevino, E. (1995). *Eukee the jumpy, jumpy elephant.* Plantation, Florida: Specialty Press.

Galvin, M. (1988). *Otto learns about his medicine.* New York, N.Y.: Magination Press.

Gordon, M. (1992). *I would if I could.* DeWitt, New York: GSI.

Gordon, M. (1991). *Jumpin' Johnny gets back to work: A child's guide to ADHD/hyperactivity.* DeWitt, New York: GSI.

Gordon, M. (1992). *My brother's a world-class pain.* DeWitt, New York: GSI.

Moss, D. (1989). *Shelly, the hyperactive turtle.* Rockville, Maryland: Woodbine House.

Quinn, P., & Stern , J. (1991). *Putting on the brakes.* New York: Magination Press.

About Associated Disorders

Ingersoll, B., & Goldstein, S. (1993). *Attention deficit disorder and learning disabilities: Realities, myths and controversial treatments.* New York: Bantam, Doubleday, Dell.

Koplewicz, H. S. (1996). *It's nobody's fault: New hope and help for difficult children and their parents.* New York: Random House.

Silver, L. (1984). *The misunderstood child: A guide for parents of learning disabled children.* New York: McGraw-Hill.

About Teaching & Developing Social Skills

McGinnis, E., & Goldstein, A. (1990). *Skillstreaming in early childhood: Teaching prosocial skills to the preschool and kindergarten child.* Champaign, Illinois: Research Press.

About ADHD Assessment & Testing

Barkely, R. (2005). *Attention deficit hyperactivity disorder (3rd edition): A clinical workbook.* New York: The Guilford Press.

Conners, C. (1997). *Conner's rating scales-revised.* North Tonawanda, New York: Multi-Health Systems.

Goyette, C, Conners, C., & Ulrich, R. (1978), Normative data on revised Conner's parent and teacher rating scales. *Journal of Abnormal Child Psychology, 6, 221-236.*

Greenberg, L. (1991). *T.O.V.A. interpretation manual: Test of variables of attention computer program,* Minneapolis, Minnesota: University of Minnesota,

Keefe, F., Kopel, S., & Gordon, S. (1978). *A practical guide to behavioral assessment.* New York: Springer.

About ADHD Behavior Management Techniques

Clark, L. (1989). *The time-out solution.* Chicago: Contemporary Books.

Kendall, P. (1988). *Stop and think workbook.* Merion Station, Pennsylvania.

Emerson, S. What ADHD is, and isn't...and what to do. *Patient Care, July 1996, 26-51.*

About Medications for ADHD

Wilens, T.. (2004). *Straight talk about psychiatric medications for kids, revised edition.* New York: The Guilford Press

Internet Sites Relating to ADHD
Note: New sites are being added, deleted, or relocated on the Internet daily. This listing is current as of the date of this book's printing.

Site Name	Internet Site Address	Comments
CHADD	http://www.chadd.org	Extensive site, info on ADHD from different sources.
myADHD.com	http://www.myadhd.com	Unique site for assessment and treatment of ADHD. Send rating scales electronically. Over 100 treatment tools.
National ADD Association	http://www.add.org	Lots of info on ADHD, including medication, support groups and links to other sites.
Learning Disabilities Association	http://www.ldanatl.org	Includes links to learning disability state associations, has info on both children and adults.
LD Online	http://www.ldonline.org	Extensive site covering all aspects of learning disabilities.
Council for Exceptional Children	http://www.cec.sped.org	Info geared toward educators of children.
Parents Helping Parents	http://www.php.com	Parents of children with a variety of disabilities, including LD and ADHD.
Matrix Parent Network	http://matrixparents.org/index.html	Support for parents of children with learning disabilities.
Childhood ADD List	Send message to: listserv@n7kbt.rain.com	A list service for parents of ADHD children.
ADD-Plus	http://www.add-plus.com	A compendium of resources for parents & teachers of ADHD kids
ADD on AOL	http://users.aol.com/jimams/addonaol.html	An ADHD resource guide, with excerpts from ADHD message boards.
ADD FAQ Site	http://www3.sympatico.ca/frankk/	A site for parents and teachers of ADHD-diagnosed children
ADHD Library	http://newideas.net/p0000374.htm	80 pages of ADHD information for parents, teachers, and professionals

Site Name	Internet Site Address	Comments
The Feingold Association of the United States	http://www.feingold.org/	Web site of the Feingold Association of the U.S., generating awareness on the potential role of food and syn thetic additives in the treatment of ADD/ADHD.
The HADD-IT Page Humorous ADDults Intriguing Themselves	http://www.busprod.com/ scurtiss/	web site of ADHD humor by those who have ADD.
Oppositional Defiant Disorder	http://www.sundial.net/ ~techman/index3.html	Info and resources on Oppositional Defiant Disorder (ODD). Gives ideas to parents and teachers for peace of mind and techniques to deal with defiant children
ADD News for Chirstian Families	http://members.aol.com/	A site for Christian families living
ADDNetUK	http://www.web-tv.co.uk/	ADHD information in UK
Tourette Syndrome Association Web Page	http://neuro-www2.mgh. harvard.edu/tsa/tsamain.nclk	Information about Tourette syndrome
NIMH Page on ADHD	http://www.nimh.nih.gov/ publicat/adhd.htm	This is a fact sheet on ADHD by The National Institute for Mental Health

APPENDIX C

Helpful Materials

Please refer to the guidelines and charts on the following pages.

Time-out Guidelines

Time-out is one of the most effective discipline methods for young children. Time-outs give kids (and parents) an opportunity to calm down and get their behavior under control. Do you know how to effectively use time-outs? The Time-out guidelines are a step-by-step reference to help you.

Drawing/Writing Activity Sheet for Time-outs

A handy sheet to help keep little minds (and hands) busy while the child stays in the time-out spot. The sheet is to help them write out or draw their feelings, or reflect on what they did wrong, or what they could do right next time.

Medication Effectiveness Report

A handy week-long checklist adapted from Dr. John Taylor's Medication Evaluation Guidelines to assist you in monitoring your child's medicated behavior. Useful for reference purposes when consulting with ADHD therapists or doctors.

Good Behavior Chart

A useful point system chart which you can use to help your ADHD child work toward selected positive behaviors. Helps the child measure his/her progress, and provides daily reinforcement of behavioral goals.

Weekday/Weekend Schedule

ADHD children respond well to routines. Use this schedule to plan out each day.

Good Behavior Contract & Reward Menus

Use the contract to help your child work toward desired behaviors, and use the reward menu as a guide for motivating your child to reach his/her goals.

Warning Labels

Help your child identify (and stay away from) dangerous items around the house by using these handy labels.

Important Questions to Ask

What do you ask when having your child assessed for ADHD? What questions do you ask when selecting a professional to do the assessment? What questions do you ask when selecting a professional to help treat your child? This helpful list reminds you of important questions to ask, and keeps you organized for your meeting with the professional or physician.

Time-Out Guidelines

- **The Basic Rules:**
  1. No getting out of the time-out chair until the timer goes off.
  2. No talking during the time-out.
  3. No watching TV during the time-out.
  4. No kicking the wall, slamming doors, screaming, or throwing things during time-out.
  5. No toys, blankets, or other play items allowed.

- **The Purpose of Time-outs:**

Time-outs give children and their parents an opportunity to calm down and get their behavior under control. Time-out is an opportunity for reflection about the misbehavior. It is a simple and *unemotional* way of correcting misbehavior. If used consistently, time-outs will train a child to stop and think first, rather than act impulsively.

- **How to Do It:**

Simply stated, time-outs work like this: when your child misbehaves, she's removed from the area and told to sit quietly for a brief period of time. This gives her and you a chance to cool off. When the time is up, she's given the opportunity to start over without further scolding.

The Chair: Pick a small chair to use exclusively for the time-outs. Place it in a quiet hallway or corner, not in the child's room or facing a window or TV. Once in the chair your child should not be allowed to move it around.

State the Problem: Young children, especially those with ADHD, often don't have any idea what they did wrong, so it's important to explain the reason for the time-out. Be short and specific. Make it clear that the child's *behavior* was the problem, *not* the child. Talk calmly. Do not get emotional. Just state your case briefly, then leave. If the child tries to engage you in conversation, ignore him and walk away.

Time: How much time should the child spend in the time-out chair? A general rule of thumb is that a time-out should last one minute for each year of a child's age (2 minutes for a two-year-old, etc). But use your best judgement and adjust the time depending on your child's temperament. Start timing as soon as your child can sit quietly in the chair. A kitchen timer with a bell is best.

Help the Child Focus: If you wish, you can help the child focus her thoughts on what she did wrong by having her draw or write out her feelings on paper while she sits on the Time-out chair. The *Drawing/Writing Activity Sheet for Time-Outs* is an ideal tool for helping your child ponder her behavior. The child could also look at *The Buzz & Pixie Activity Coloring Book*.

Hugs: When the time-out ends, don't scold or be angry. The child needs a hug and a chance to show good behavior and start over.

Be Consistent: Decide ahead of time which misbehaviors merit a time-out, and which ones do not. Use time-outs at home as well as in public. Use the same routine for each time-out. And never get emotional!

- **What if the Child Won't Stay Put?**

If your child refuses to go to the time-out chair, don't lose your cool. Take hold of her and firmly sit her down. If she gets up, calmly put her back in the chair. Stand there and hold her, if necessary, until the timer goes off. Some kids will sit for the required time but refuse to calm down, yelling, crying or kicking. Tell the child that if she refuses to be quiet, you will double her time. If that fails, end the time-out when the timer rings, but take away a privilege.

Summarized from *The Fine Art of the Time-Out*, in Parenting Magazine, Nov. 1996, pp. 170-175. Article adapted from the book, *The Time-Out Prescription*, by Donna G. Corwin, Contemporary Books, Inc., 1996.

Drawing/Writing Activity Sheet for Time-outs

While your child is taking a time-out, have him draw out his feelings, or depict what he did wrong, or what he could have done right. Discuss the picture after the time-out is over.

Medication Effectiveness Report

Child's Name: _____   Medication: _____

Dosage: _____   For the Week of _____

Weekly Rating of DESIRED EFFECTS of Medication

Scoring: A = Excellent (very pleasant)   D = Poor (unpleasant)

            B = Good (okay, livable)   F = Failure (intolerable)

            C = Fair (barely toler able)

TRAITS	MON	TUE	WED	THU	FRI	SAT	SUN
Activity Control: Mouth, hands and feet are well controlled; sits for normal length of time; not fidgety or squirmy; does not poke, touch and grab.							
Brain is in Gear: Asks thoughtful questions; understands and remembers clearly; not absent-minded; seems "tuned-in."							
Conscience: Considers moral aspects of decisions; doesn't lie, cheat or steal; respects boundaries; asks permission before doing things; is repentant and apologetic if caught in a misdeed.							
Diligence: Does things without being reminded or nagged; careful rather than careless; wants to do a good job; volunteers to help; wants things to be orderly.							
Emotional Control: Shows patience; is not easily upset; doesn't have temper tantrums; takes frustrations in stride.							
Focusing: Has normal attention span; pursues goals without being side-tracked; completes activities; does not move from one unfinished activity to another; not distractible.							
Gentleness: Is polite, generous, courteous, doesn't demand his own way or argue; is obedient and cooperative; respects authority.							

Weekly Rating of UNDESIRED EFFECTS of Medication

Scoring: 0 = Not Occurring   1 = Mild/Very Slight   3 = Moderate, but acceptable

            4= Severe, cannot allow to continue

UNDESIRED EFFECTS	MON	TUE	WED	THU	FRI	SAT	SUN
Groggy, overly tired							
Irritable, cries easily							
Headaches							
Nervous Tics, Jerky muscles							
Appetite decreases							
Doesn't fall asleep easily							
Other (Describe)							

Good Behavior Chart

Child's Name: _____   **Week of:** _____ **to** _____

MY GOAL: **By the End of the Week, I will earn** _____ **points!**

DESIRED BEHAVIOR	WEEKLY SCORESHEET - POINTS EARNED						
	MON	TUE	WED	THU	FRI	SAT	SUN
Behavior # 1							
Behavior # 2							
Behavior # 3							
Behavior # 4							
TOTAL POINTS							

NOTE: In the space for describing desired behavior, you can write out the description of the desired behavior you want your child to achieve. Better yet, you or the child could draw a picture of the child doing that good behavior (e.g., sharing)

PARENT'S REMINDER:

Daily rewards for good behavior: _____

End-of-the-week reward for achieving point goal: _____

Consequences for unacceptable behavior: _____

Weekday/Weekend Schedule

Children thrive on consistent, established routines. Having a written daily schedule will ensure that desired behaviors will occur. We provide you with one example below for reference.

(EXAMPLE SCHEDULE)

TIME	SCHEDULED ACTIVITY
7:00 am	Wake up, Make bed, Get dressed.
7:30 am	Eat Breakfast, brush teeth & hair.
8:00 am	Go to school
12:00 noon	Come and eat lunch
1:00 pm	Practice drawing/Playing with Legos, etc.
2:00 pm	Go outside (i.e., to the park, go bike riding, go swimming, etc.)
4:00 pm	Return home, watch cartoons.
5:00 pm	Eat dinner
6:00 pm	Clean up, brush teeth, take a bath, change into pajamas
7:00 pm	Quiet play and/or storytime
8:00 pm	Prepare school clothes for next day, Tuck into bed, lights out

Use the following blank schedule sheet to plan your child's daily routine:

TIME	SCHEDULED ACTIVITY
7:00 am	
7:30 am	
8:00 am	
8:30 am	
9:00 am	
10:00 am	
11:00 am	
12:00 noon	
1:00 pm	
2:00 pm	
3:00 pm	
4:00 pm	
5:00 pm	
6:00 pm	
7:00 pm	
8:00 pm	
9:00 pm	

From: ADHD in the Young Child by C. L. Reimers and B. A. Brunger. (Specialty Press, 1999). Limited copes may be made for personal use.

Good Behavior Contract

Here is a sample format of a simple behavior contract you can make with your child. Talk about a behavior you want to reinforce or eliminate and write it out simply with your child. Specify a reward if the child keeps his/her promise and sign it together.

SAMPLE CONTRACT

I, <u>BUZZ</u>, AGREE TO <u>STOP HITTING MY SISTER, PIXIE.</u>
IF I KEEP MY PROMISE TODAY, <u>I CAN CHOOSE A REWARD FROM THE REWARD MENU AT THE END OF THE DAY.</u>

CHILD'S SIGNATURE : <u>XXXXXX</u>

PARENT'S SIGNATURE : <u>MOM and/or DAD</u>

DATE : <u>XXXXXXX</u>

CONTRACT

I, _____ , AGREE TO _____.

IF I KEEP MY PROMISE TODAY,

_____.

CHILD'S SIGNATURE : _____

PARENT'S SIGNATURE : _____

DATE : _____

Reward Menus

Together with your child, agree on a list of rewards which the child can earn for good behavior. You could simply list the rewards, or perhaps assign a point value next to each reward, and use the Good Behavior Chart to record points as the child works toward the goal.

(Sample Reward Menu)

REWARD	POINTS NEEDED
Buy a Lego Castle Set	50 Points
Buy an Action Figure	45 Points
Go to the Movies	40 Points
Go to the Museum	35 Points
Have a Friend Sleep Over	30 Points
Go Get Ice Cream	25 Points
Buy a New Game	20 Points
Buy a Book	15 Points
Make a Cake	10 Points
Have a Special Meal	5 Points

Other Ideas for Rewards:

1. **Foods**: Tacos, Spaghetti, Pizza, Candy, Soda, Cookies, Brownies, Gum, Potato Chips, etc.

2. **Outings:** The Park, The Grocery Store, The Mall, Aquariums, Exhibits, Amusement Parks, Fairs & Carnivals, Field Trips, Visiting Relatives, Eat out at a Restaurant, Go to an Arcade, etc.

3. **Prizes**: Dolls, Toy Cars, Toy Airplanes, Puzzles, Paint Sets, Play Dough, Stickers, Toy Candy Dispensers, Playing Cards, Videos, Electronic Games, Articles of Clothing, Award Ribbons, etc.

WARNING LABELS

To impress your child with the importance of safety in your home, you can take a tour of your house with your child and have your child affix these labels on household items.

DON'T TOUCH!		**DON'T TOUCH!**	
DON'T TOUCH!		**DON'T TOUCH!**	
DON'T OPEN!		**DON'T OPEN!**	
DON'T OPEN!		**DON'T OPEN!**	
POISON		**POISON**	
POISON		**POISON**	

From: ADHD in the Young Child by C. L. Reimers and B. A. Brunger. (Specialty Press, 1999). Limited copes may be made for personal use.

Important Questions to Ask

• Questions to ask yourself before having your child assessed for ADHD:

1. Why do I want an assessment for my child? Why do I think my child may have ADHD?
2. What should be included in the assessment?
3. What qualifications do I want the professional to have?
4. Will my insurance cover the cost of the assessment and treatment?
5. Are there any other unusual events or circumstances happening in our family that may be affecting my child?

• Questions to ask the professional before having your child assessed for ADHD:

1. What credentials/training have you had in assessing ADHD? How long have you been doing assessments?
2. What experience have you had with testing students of my child's age?
3. Before the assessment, can I have a written plan of what you will do and what the results will tell me?
4. How should I prepare my child for the assessment?
5. Will the assessment include all of the tests required by public schools so that my child will be considered for receiving services?
6. What can I expect in terms of a written report at the end of the assessment?
7. How much will the assessment cost?
8. How do you diagnose for ADHD?
9. Which types of tests or measurements do you use? Do you use the DSM-IV or other reference(s)?
10. How long will the assessment take?
11. Do other professionals assist in the assessment process?
12. Are you knowledgeable about special services provided at public schools for children with ADHD?

• Questions to ask after the assessment:

1. Were the assessment report results clear? If not, did the professional answer all of my questions?
2. What did the professional recommend for my child based on these test results?
3. Does the report show strengths and weaknesses in a way that you can learn and use the information?
4. Did you obtain suggestions on ways to overcome some of the effects of areas of difficulty?
5. Did you determine that the symptoms exist in at least two settings (home, school, etc.)?
6. Was this professional easy to talk to? Were all my questions answered satisfactorily?

• **Questions to ask yourself before searching for counseling or treatment:**

1. What issues do I want addressed?
2. How can I prepare my child for counseling or treatment?
3. Would my child be better in an individual or group setting?
4. What are my expectations of the counseling experience or treatment?
5. Am I willing to be part of the counseling sessions if asked?
6. Am I willing to make the time and financial commitment required?

• **Questions to ask the physician or counseling professional/therapist who may do treatment:**

1. What approach do you take for treating ADHD? Is counseling part of your treatment plan?
2. How is medication used in your practice?
3. If medication is prescribed, what might be some of the side effects?
4. What other therapy in addition to medication would you suggest?
5. If I decide not to put my child on medication, would you attempt to find other possible solutions?
6. What are some typical results you have had with your clients? Could you arrange for me to speak with some of them?
7. What are your fees? Do you have a sliding scale?
8. What can I do at home to help my child?
9. What is the format of the counseling sessions?
10. What are the goals of the treatment or counseling sessions?
11. Will the sessions be time-limited or are they continuous as needed?
12. Would my child be working with you, or are there other counselors?
13. What is your experience in working with ADHD children? What are your credentials? What licenses or certificates do you have?
14. How long do you think the counseling/treatment sessions will last?
15. How does this counselor/physician/therapist answer my questions relative to other professionals I have spoken to?

• **Questions to ask yourself before deciding to search for a private school:**

1. What are my child's academic, social and learning styles?
2. Under what conditions does my child learn best: noise level, number of students, length of class sessions, single teacher vs. staff?
3. What extracurricular activities does my child enjoy?
4. Is it important for me that the private school be accredited?
5. What services or accommodations will my child need?

• **Questions to ask when selecting a private school:**

1. What are your admissions requirements?
2. What are your annual costs? Do you offer scholarships or financial aid?

3. What is your average class size for my child's grade?
4. Are all your teachers credentialed? How many have special education credentials?
5. What training have your teachers had relating to strategies for working with students with learning disabilities?
6. How many aides are there in each classroom?
7. Do you have counseling services? Tutoring?
8. What is your school's expectations of parents? Do you encourage parents to visit the classrooms?
9. What is your school's discipline policy? How do you work to modify student behavior?
10. What extracurricular activities are offered?
11. Did the school representative answer all my questions satisfactorily?
12. How does this school compare to other schools I have looked at?

• **Questions to ask when selecting an educational therapist:**

1. Do I know the difference between an educational therapist and a tutor?
2. Do I know my child's learning style?
3. Does my child have a preference between a male or female therapist?
4. Do I want the therapist to work with my child's teacher at school?
5. Is the educational therapist a member of the Association of Educational Therapists?
6. Is the therapist's services different from those of a tutor?
7. What training does the educational therapist have with children my child's age?
8. What is the educational therapist's fee structure?
9. How long are the sessions? How long does the educational therapist expect to work with my child?
10. Does the educational therapist have frequent review sessions with parents?
11. How will the educational therapist use my child's specific learning style to develop compensatory strategies?
12. Would the educational therapist be willing to attend an IEP meeting?
13. Did the educational therapist answer all of my questions?
14. How does this educational therapist compare with others I have spoken to?

APPENDIX D

Fun Stuff for Kids

Finger Puppets

You can make photocopies of the finger puppet sheet, have your child color them, and cut them out. Use these finger puppets to re-enact the situations depicted in the cartoon section at the end of this book, or use them to role-play new situations.

Buzz & Pixie Game: Catch Me Doing Good!

You can make photocopies of the game board and the game cards to play a short, simple game to reinforce positive behavior.

Puzzles for Fidgety Moments

Several puzzles you can photocopy and use for quiet activities.

Motivational Posters

Photocopy these posters and have your child color them and hang them up to remind the child of positive behaviors.

Finger Puppets

Buzz

Pixie

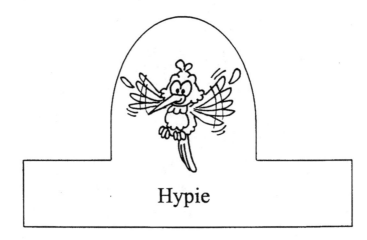

Hypie

Buzz & Pixie Game: Catch Me Doing Good!

Help Buzz and Pixie get through a day by being good! Take turns rolling dice and moving your Buzz or Pixie token along the squares. Choose a card when you land on a marked space, and answer what you would do if you were Buzz or Pixie.

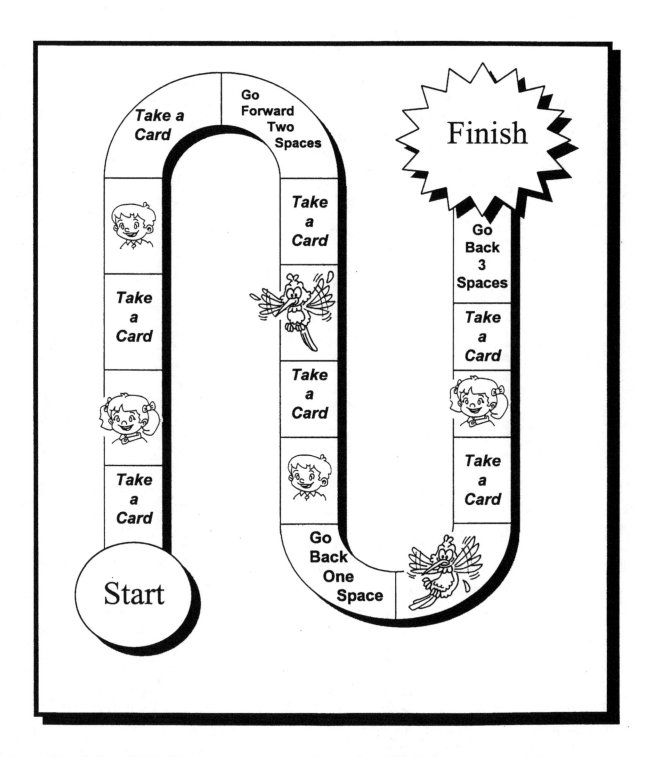

From: ADHD in the Young Child by C. L. Reimers and B. A. Brunger. (Specialty Press, 1999). Limited copes may be mpade for personal use.

Buzz & Pixie Game: Catch Me Doing Good!

Game Cards, Tokens and Dice for you to photocopy, color and cut out for use.

You wake up early in the morning, but mommy and daddy are still asleep. What should you do? (Then move ahead one space)	Tell about two things you can do today to help your mommy and daddy. (Then move your token ahead two spaces.)
Tell what you would do if someone teases you at school. (Then move your token ahead two spaces.)	You're playing with a friend. She takes one of your toys. What would you say? (Then move your token ahead one space.)
When you feel wiggly or silly, what can you do to help you calm down? (Then move your token ahead one space.)	What are some good things you can do when you go shopping with mommy or daddy? (Then move your token ahead two spaces.)
What are some good things you can do when you visit someone's house? (Then move your token ahead two spaces.)	What are some good things you can do when you go eat at a restaurant? (Then move your token ahead one space.)

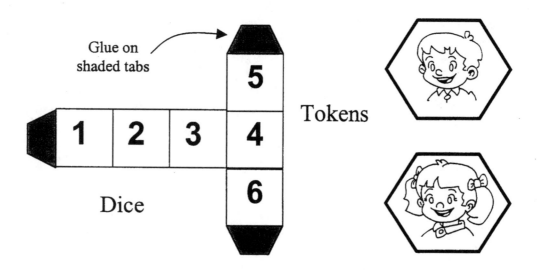

Glue on shaded tabs

Dice

Tokens

Puzzles for Fidgety Moments

Photocopy these puzzles for quiet activities.

Puzzles for Fidgety Moments

Photocopy these puzzles for quiet activities.

Winnie the Pooh Word Search

```
C  R  Y  E  N  O  H  C  P  M  P
T  H  O  I  H  P  A  O  S  T  I
I  C  R  O  N  R  O  L  D  I  G
G  R  L  I  R  H  T  T  O  B  L
G  O  Z  O  S  B  F  V  O  B  E
E  W  T  O  V  T  O  E  W  A  T
R  S  W  V  B  W  O  U  E  R  J
P  L  A  G  N  A  K  P  N  R  V
G  A  R  D  E  N  X  L  H  C  T
E  E  Y  O  R  E  V  A  V  E  E
F  R  I  E  N  D  S  Y  Z  D  R
```

Try to find these words:

BOUNCE	ROO
CARROTS	TIGGER
CROWS	TREE
EEYORE	WOODS
FRIENDS	OWL
GARDEN	HONEY
KANGA	PIGLET
PLAY	POOH
RABBIT	
CHRISTOPHER	

Zoo Animal Word Search

```
B  E  B  E  N  V  X  Q  C  R  A
U  I  L  E  P  W  I  O  E  L  L
L  X  R  E  A  A  W  E  L  I  A
Y  R  E  D  P  R  D  I  O  B  R
E  E  I  S  S  H  G  N  H  X  B
K  G  L  R  A  A  A  F  G  X  E
N  I  P  M  T  C  H  N  I  I  Z
O  T  A  O  A  Q  J  O  T  S  P
M  L  R  M  L  L  Z  I  R  C  H
L  A  E  T  U  R  T  L  E  S  X
C  L  G  I  R  A  F  F  E  U  E
```

Try to find these words:

APE	ELEPHANT
BEAR	LLAMA
BIRDS	MONKEY
DEER	PIG
COW	TIGER
CAMEL	TURTLE
FISH	ZEBRA
LION	
HORSE	
GIRAFFE	
ALLIGATOR	

From: ADHD in the Young Child by C. L. Reimers and B. A. Brunger. (Specialty Press, 1999). Limited copes may be made for personal use.

Motivational Posters

Photocopy these posters and have your child color them and hang them up to remind the child of positive behaviors.